D0049223

Final Call

Final
Call

STEVEN J. LAWSON

CROSSWAY BOOKS • WHEATON, ILLINOIS
A DIVISION OF GOOD NEWS PUBLISHERS

Final Call

Copyright © 1994 by Steven J. Lawson

Published by Crossway Books
        a division of Good News Publishers
        1300 Crescent Street
        Wheaton, Illinois 60187

Cover design: Dennis Hill

First printing 1994

Printed in the United States of America

ISBN 0-89107-796-0

Library of Congress Cataloging-in-Publication Data
Lawson, Steven J.
    Final call, etc. / Steven J. Lawson.
        p.   cm.
      1. Bible. N.T. Revelation I-III—Criticism, interpretation, etc.
2. United States—Religion—1960- 3. Repentance—Christianity
I. Title.
BS2825.2.L294 1994   228'.06—dc20   94-7174
ISBN 0-89107-796-0

01		00		99		98		97		96		95		94
15	14	13	12	11	10	9	8	7	6	5	4	3	2	1

I dedicate this book to my precious wife,
Anne,
God's perfect gift for me,
who has faithfully stood beside me
and unfailingly encouraged me in my ministry.

Together, we share the burden
of the message of this book.

"An excellent wife, who can find?
For her worth is far above jewels."

PROVERBS 31:10

ACKNOWLEDGMENTS

I feel compelled to publicly thank a special group of people who helped make this book a reality. I want to thank: Todd Murray and Jeff Kinley, two fellow pastors with whom I have served together in the same church for over a decade, for their wealth of creative genius; Bill Eubanks, a pastor I discipled years ago who has long since exceeded my ministry, for reviewing my manuscript with a keen theological mind; Sherry Humphres, my secretary, who tirelessly typed this manuscript; my wife, Anne, to whom I dedicate this book, whose sensitivity to the Holy Spirit led her to encourage me to write this book.

CONTENTS

FOREWORD

WHAT POSSIBLE RELEVANCE to modern Christians could there be in a series of messages written to seven churches in Asia Minor at the end of the first century (recorded in Revelation 2–3)?

First of all, the messages come from the glorified Lord Jesus Himself. They are His last words to the church before the New Testament canon was closed.

Second, the problems and issues those churches were struggling with are precisely the same matters that trouble the church today.

Steven J. Lawson believes our Lord's words to the seven churches of Asia Minor are a fitting wake-up call for the church in our age. Carefully drawing the parallels between the first-century church and the church of our day, he shows how these timeless messages still speak to us with supreme relevance.

This is the best kind of Bible teaching—true to the text, faithful to the historical context, while bringing the message emphatically into the practical here-and-now.

And the message is inescapable. If our society is ever to awaken out of the spiritual and moral malaise that has set in, the church of Jesus Christ must awaken first.

Final Call is a passionate appeal for the church to wake up spiritually. Poignantly, powerfully, Lawson pleads his case directly from Scripture. What he says is both a serious indictment of the modern church and a heartfelt, loving entreaty for believers, based on the words of our Lord Himself.

If your heart responds at all to the Lordship of Christ, you will be moved by this book. It is a message that calls for the deepest possible reflection, the most intense kind of self-examination, and the most faithful, humble obedience.

I am extremely grateful for this book. It is precisely the kind of book we need more of. Its message is biblical. It exalts Christ. It boldly declares truth. It offers immediate practical applications. And it provokes the reader to a deeper love for his Lord.

My prayer for you as you turn the page and begin reading is that God will use this book to summon you to the kind of commitment Jesus was calling for when He first spoke these messages to the beloved apostle so many years ago.

John F. MacArthur, Jr.

PREFACE

SOMETHING HAS GONE WRONG IN AMERICA.

Desperately wrong.

By outward appearances, America is healthy. Prosperous. Educated. Thriving. Our economy is recovering. Our technology is advancing. Our exports are increasing.

But inwardly, the soul of America is dying. Our country is suffering from acute heart failure. Our pulse for God is weakening. Our arteries of religious faith are blocked. We need emergency open-heart surgery. A spiritual bypass.

Better yet, we need a new heart.

I see America through the eyes of Little Rock, Arkansas. And recently, what I have seen greatly disturbs me. During the last thirteen years of my pastorate here, I have witnessed firsthand an incredible phenomenon—the meteoric rise of President Bill Clinton. I have seen up close the making of a President.

Mr. Clinton ran for the White House on a platform of change. A change in national ideology. A change in political agenda. A change in social direction. And, unfortunately, at its very core, a change in the moral foundation of America.

True to his campaign promises, President Clinton has ushered in sweeping change. On January 23, 1993—the third day of his presidency—Clinton issued five executive orders that signaled the changes to come. He initiated the lifting of the ban on homosexuals in the military. He ordered the ban on fetal tissue to be lifted. He ordered the ban on abortion counseling in federally-funded clinics to be lifted. He ordered the process of approving the importation of the abortion-inducing medication RU-486 to begin. He ordered funds for abortions in military hospitals overseas to be paid for by U.S. taxpayers.

All these in only the first three days!

Is this the kind of change that we need? More grisly abortions? The proliferation of "safe sex"? Pro-homosexuality in the military? The appalling redefinition of child pornography? The increased taxation of families? Is this the change America needs?

I think not.

At the deepest level, our national problems are spiritual. Not economic. Not medical. Not educational. We need more than legislative or social change. These are fine and good, but they don't go far enough. We need a spiritual change of heart. Only spiritual solutions can solve our deepest problems.

True change must come from within. A change from the inside out. A change of heart.

So, who *can* bring about such a spiritual change? Who *can* change our country's heart and soul?

The answer lies with the *church* of Jesus Christ. The only hope for spiritual change in America is found with God's people. God's church is the agent of change in any culture, His instrument of transforming a nation.

But, like the world around us, the soul of the American church is dying. *Our* pulse for God is weakening. *Our* arteries of faith have become blocked. *We* need a spiritual bypass!

If we are to have revival in America, it must begin in the church. America's crisis will be solved only when revival catches fire in the church and spreads across the land.

As we progress into a post-Christian America, never before have we so desperately needed the church to be the church. The hope of America lies not in the White House, nor with Wall Street, but with the church of Jesus Christ.

This book is intended to be a wake-up call to the sleeping church of America. We will rediscover a vision of our glorious Lord and examine the seven letters of Jesus Christ (Revelation 1–3), written to the church 2,000 years ago in a similar hour of crisis. We've heard from the experts. The politicians. The media. The church consultants. Now, it's time to hear from Jesus Christ Himself.

It's time to hear His *final call!*

STEVEN J. LAWSON
Little Rock, Arkansas

THE LORDSHIP OF JESUS CHRIST

REVELATION 1

I

IT'S MIDNIGHT AGAIN!

Revelation 1:1–11

THE CALL HAD TO GO OUT.

The hour was *desperate*.

With British ships anchored in the harbor under the protective cloak of night, the city of Boston slept. Unaware. Unsuspecting. Defenseless. A young nation's destiny hung in the balance.

As the city lay in a state of siege, Boston was overflowing with British troops ready to attack. A nation conceived in freedom seemed aborted before she could even be born.

Deep into the chilly night of April 18, 1775, 700 British soldiers marched secretly through the streets of Boston, advancing to the riverfront. There, they were to board small boats and row across the Charles River to launch a surprise attack on Lexington and Concord. The future of America looked as dark as the midnight sky overhead.

But while all Boston slept, one man kept watch. Remaining alert in the still of the night. Wide-eyed to the approaching dangers at hand. Paul Revere refused to sleep.

Across town, Dr. Joseph Warren was directing the patriot activities in Boston. He knew a messenger must be sent at once to warn Lexington. A man of great courage. More committed to the cause than to his own life. So he sent for Paul Revere, a forty-year-old silversmith.

The plan was simple. It called for Revere to row ahead of the

British troops and ride through the night to Lexington and Concord to warn the sleeping citizens of the approaching danger.

The call had to go out.

Without hesitating, and with the fate of the young nation resting on his strong shoulders, Revere dashed off to the Old North Church. Daringly, with British soldiers asleep upstairs in the church, he awakened the sexton. "Two lanterns in the belfry," he whispered in a hushed breathless tone. "Now!"

The signal would be recognized by patriots across the river in Charleston. Two if by sea. That meant the British would be coming that very night by boat. Rushing home to tell his family good-bye—perhaps for the last time—Revere hurried to the waterfront. There, two friends promised to help row him to the other side.

With muffled oars, they slithered past an English man-o'-war, the *Somerset*, patroling the river. Passing under the noses of 64 British cannons, Revere slipped by, just slightly ahead of the British troops.

They landed in the shadows on the other side. Safely. Men from Charleston had seen the signal and had a fast horse saddled and waiting.

And off he rode. Coattails flapping in the wind. Hair flowing in the dark night. Perspiration beading on his brow. Paul Revere stopped at every farmhouse village along the way. With horse hooves skidding to a halt, Revere rushed up to each house and pounded on the door, calling out, "The British are coming! Wake up! The enemy is upon you!"

All along the way, Minutemen rallied and answered the call. True to their name, they came running the minute they heard the call. Muskets were fired into the sky. Church bells began ringing. The call was relayed far and wide by each man.

All went well. That is, until two English officers spotted Revere. One tried to ride ahead of Paul. The other attempted to overtake him from behind.

But to no avail. Revere cut quickly through a field, galloped past a muddy pond, and found another road to Lexington. As if riding a horse of destiny, nothing could stop him now.

The call had to go out.

Approaching hoofbeats on the cobbled stones of Lexington signaled his arrival. Urgently, Revere began beating on doors. With a loud voice that pierced the cool night air, he shouted, "To arms! To arms! The British are coming! The British are coming!"

Immediately, candles were lit. Windows flew open. Curtains were flung back. Heads peered out. And men dressed quickly. Each Minuteman grabbed his musket and awakened his neighbor. Shots were fired into the night air. Torches were lit.

No time to sleep!

By early morning, area farmers were gathered on Lexington Green. Fifty to 60 Minutemen were rallied, armed, and positioned to stand against the approaching British. They were ready to *die* for the cause of freedom and to defend their families.

As redcoats marched onto Lexington Green, the first shots of the Revolutionary War were fired. The war had now begun.

In the skirmishes of the day, the colonists lost 93 men at Lexington and Concord. But, far worse, the English lost the lives of 273 soldiers. The die had been cast. A statement made. This was America's war to win. And it all started on the hot heels of Paul Revere's famous ride for freedom.

The midnight ride of Paul Revere was a daring dash through the countryside of America to wake up a young, sleeping nation. It was a call to action. A call to bear arms. A call to stand and fight.

As the future of America hung precariously in the balance and the destiny of this nation lay in jeopardy, one man sounded the alarm and changed the outcome of the war. On that dark night, with hope all but extinguished, the call was sounded and the course of this nation was dramatically altered.

It's midnight again.

And history *must* repeat itself.

An enemy more dangerous than British redcoats has dropped its anchors in our harbors and has landed on our shores. Our cities are surrounded. Our freedoms are endangered. Our national security is at risk.

This invading army is waging a bitter war for the very soul of America. We are deeply entrenched in a spiritual war of values. We are engaged in a cultural war over morality. A life and death struggle for the family is raging. An invisible war for the very fiber and foundation of our society is escalating. At stake is the future of America.

No arena is left untouched. Every institution is a battlefield. This war is being fought in the media, in the classrooms, and in the legislative halls of our country. It is being staged in the courtrooms, in the universities, and in the marketplaces of our land. Every square inch and every second in time is a context of war.

This hostile army has even marched into our *churches*. It has battered down our front doors and invaded our sanctuaries. Its soldiers have pitched their tents in our pews. Some even occupy our pulpits. The church is under siege.

Who is this enemy? What foe could have the troops, the resources, and the strategy to accomplish such a massive invasion? What opposing army could put our nation in such jeopardy?

I'm talking about our greatest enemy. The Adversary. The Evil One. I'm talking about Satan himself. Once again, America is under attack! An attack that is sinister, diabolical, and hellish. And, most of all, deadly. The hour is desperate. And the future of America hangs in the balance.

The call must go out *again*.

The future of America is dependent upon one army. Only one army has the firepower to halt this enemy's aggression. Only one army can successfully defend the people and preserve our freedoms. That army is the blood-bought church of Jesus Christ. She alone is armed and equipped for the spiritual warfare at hand. She alone possesses the spiritual armor, the weapons, and the forces necessary to win this war.

But, tragically, the church is asleep. Like America on the night of Paul Revere's fateful ride, the church is sound asleep. She is comfortably tucked into bed in the pews. Covers are pulled over her head. Curtains are drawn over the stained-glass windows. Darkness fills the sanctuary. The church is fast asleep, oblivious to the enemy's approach. Unaware of the danger at hand. Slumbering. Snoring. Even dreaming.

It's midnight again.

And, once more, *the call* must go out.

But this call is different. It is not one to be sounded to the citizens of America indiscriminately. Rather, it is a call to the *churches* of our land. It is an urgent call to sleeping saints everywhere to wake up and prepare for war!

Now, more than ever, the church of Jesus Christ must answer our Lord's final call. Martin Luther's words that rang so loudly through the Reformation must ring across our land today: *Let the church be the church!* The body of Christ, like a mighty army, must rise up and meet the crisis of the hour.

This book will take you on a midnight ride through the churches of America. Its message is pounding on the front door of every sanctuary. Its hands are cupped and calling out to every pastor. Its musket is fired into the night air to wake up every congregation. It is a call to repentance. A call to obedience. A call to stand and fight.

With a voice like a mighty trumpet, our Lord is calling out to His churches across the land. With nail-pierced hands cupped, riding a white steed at full gallop, He is sending out His call far and wide to every church, every pastor, and every believer.

Hear His *final call!*

Our Lord's final call—recorded in Revelation 2—3—is His last word to the church. Here is the last message that He gave to the church. His final call—found in the last book of the Bible, the book of Revelation—issues our Lord's final marching orders for His army. Contained in the opening chapters of Revelation is His battle strategy for the church in the last days.

The end of this age is swiftly approaching. The sand is running short in God's hourglass. No one really knows, but this could be the final call of the final call. With a deep sense of urgency, we must hear Christ's final call to the church.

Before we examine the call itself—the seven letters to the seven churches (Revelation 2—3)—we want to see, first, the nature of the call itself (Revelation 1:1-11). Then we will see *who* it is that calls (Revelation 1:12-16) and what must be our appropriate response (Revelation 1:17-20).

But, first, what is the nature of this call? When was it given? What were its circumstances? To whom was it given? Where was it given? And what does it say to the church today?

The answers to these questions are critical. What follows are the components of the *final call* of our Lord Jesus Christ.

A SOVEREIGN CALL

This final call comes from our Sovereign Lord Himself. It comes down from heaven, from the very throne of God. Consequently, this call comes with the supreme authority of the One who sits upon the universe's throne. Because God is sovereign and rules over all, this call must be answered and obeyed.

> *The Revelation of Jesus Christ, which God gave Him to show to His bond-servants, the things which must shortly take place; and He sent and communicated it by His angel to His bond-servant John, who bore witness to the word of God and to the testimony of Jesus Christ, even to all that he saw (Revelation 1:1-2).*

Essentially, this call is "the Revelation of Jesus Christ." It is the unveiling of a Person—the Lord Jesus Christ. It is the uncovering of His divine glory and majesty. It displays His sovereign power and authority.

The channels of relaying this sovereign call are several-fold. According to these verses, it comes from God, to Christ, to an angel, to John, to the church. In other words, God gave it to His Son, who gave it to an angel, who gave it to John, who then wrote it down in a book—the book of Revelation—and sent it to seven churches in his day. Ultimately, this call has come down to the church today.

In Revelation, God unveils "the things which must shortly take place"—with emphasis upon "*must.*" It discloses events that must take place in the future. It records end-time events that God has predestined and foreordained to occur. God alone reigns in absolute sovereignty and thus possesses the all-power and all-authority needed to bring it to pass.

Rightly did A. W. Pink write, "Divine sovereignty means that God is God in fact, as well in name, that He is on the throne of the universe, directing all things, working all things 'after the counsel of His own will' (Ephesians 1:11)."

It is this Sovereign God who calls His church! God is God. He does as He pleases, only as He pleases, always as He pleases. He is the Supreme Being, and therefore the Sovereign of the universe.

What John writes in Revelation is, by his own admission, "the word of God."

This is God's Word, not John's. Here is one of the great mysteries of Scripture—how God used sinful, fallible men to write His holy, infallible Word. "All Scripture is inspired by God" (2 Timothy

3:16), meaning it is "God-breathed." It is the very breath of God, and it comes to us with sovereign authority. To obey this call is to obey God. The book of Revelation is also "the testimony of Jesus Christ." What God says, Christ says. God's Word is Christ's testimony.

This sovereign call is never optional. It is non-negotiable. Authoritative. Binding. The very Word of God. It demands complete obedience. It calls for undivided allegiance. It is our Sovereign Lord who calls.

> *Blessed is he who reads and those who hear the words of the prophecy, and heed the things which are written in it; for the time is near (Revelation 1:3).*

Answering God's call *always* leads to blessing. At the very outset of the book of Revelation, God promises a special blessing to those who read, hear, and obey its message. "He who reads" (singular) is the pastor or teacher who teaches this book. "Those who hear" (plural) are those who sit under the Word and obey its message.

Many ignore or neglect Revelation, assuming it is too hard to understand. They view it like Churchill viewed the Russians—a riddle wrapped up in a mystery inside an enigma. But God promises a special blessing to those who answer its call.

Others say, "Revelation? How irrelevant can you get?" They think this book is so futuristic that it's of no present value. Not so. This book is very relevant and practical for today. In fact, our greatest spiritual need is to know Jesus Christ. And no book so reveals His majesty as does Revelation.

Those who answer the final call are unusually *"blessed."* They experience the rich spiritual blessings that are available in Christ alone. This includes happiness, fulfillment, and satisfaction. Moreover, this blessedness refers to the fullness of God's presence, power, and peace in our lives. This is a life-changing call!

> *John to the seven churches that are in Asia: Grace to you and peace, from Him who is and who was and who is to come; and from the seven Spirits who are before His throne; and from Jesus Christ, the faithful witness, the first-born of the dead, and the ruler of the kings of the earth (Revelation 1:4-5a).*

Specifically, this call promises God's grace and peace. These two words—"grace" and "peace"—summarize all the spiritual riches that are ours in Christ. Grace is God's unmerited favor bestowed upon undeserving sinners that elevates us to the place of His blessing. All the Christian life operates by grace. We were *saved* by grace (Ephesians 2:8; Titus 3:7), we *grow* by grace (1 Corinthians 15:10), and we are *empowered* by grace (2 Corinthians 12:9). Thus, grace is not a one-time event, but is what drives the entire Christian life (1 Peter 1:2).

Because of God's grace, we have His peace. This is peace *with* God and the peace *of* God. Once enemies of God, we are now at peace with Him through Christ (Romans 5:1, 10). Our faith in Christ brings us the peace of God—an inner calmness and a supernatural tranquility of heart (Philippians 4:7).

All this comes from God. Grace and peace come from *God the Father* "who is and who was and who is to come"—past, present, and future. In eternity past, He chose us to be the recipients of His sovereign grace (Ephesians 1:3-4). In the present, He pours out grace and peace to us (2 Thessalonians 3:16; James 4:6). In the future, He will continue to give us His grace and peace throughout all eternity. This grace and peace is mediated from the Father into our lives through "the seven Spirits who are before His throne"—*God the Holy Spirit*.

Additionally, *God the Son*, Jesus Christ is the source of grace and peace. As "the faithful witness," He preached grace and peace (John 4:10). As "the first-born of the dead," He died and rose again to provide it (Romans 5:1, 11). As "the ruler of the kings of the earth," He is enthroned at God's right hand to dispense it as it pleases Him (John 14:27).

All three members of the Godhead—Father, Son, Holy Spirit—work together to minister grace and peace to us. Like three mighty rivers flowing together into one mighty ocean of blessing, the Trinity is pouring out their grace and peace into our lives.

> *To Him who loves us, and released us from our sins by His blood, and He has made us to be a kingdom, priests to His God and Father; to Him be the glory and the dominion forever and ever. Amen (Revelation 1:5b-6).*

In John's day, the individual counted for nothing. Kings counted. The state counted. Caesar counted. But the oppressed millions of the Roman Empire were mere chattel. Yet, with Christ, they counted for everything! He loves His church deeply. At best, a mother loves her child in only a limited way. A husband loves his wife in only a limited way. But Christ loves us perfectly.

This love was supremely displayed at the cross. There, Jesus died and "released us from our sins by His blood." With one mighty atoning work, Jesus freed us from our sins (John 8:36). The blood of Christ—shed once and for all time—paid the full purchase price to obtain our release. We have been "justified by His blood" (Romans 5:9).

By virtue of His death, Christ has made us to be "a kingdom." In John's day, Roman citizenship was for the privileged few. The great masses of the Empire were mere slaves and subjects. But in Christ, believers are made citizens of a heavenly kingdom and are given great spiritual privileges (Philippians 3:20; Ephesians 2:19). Think of it! Ordinary fishermen like John—and tax-gatherers, harlots, and great sinners like you and me—were made distinguished citizens of heaven.

Jesus has also made us to be "priests to His God." As priests, we have privileged access to come boldly into God's presence. And we are to be channels through whom He works in this world (1 Peter 2:5-9). Consequently, to Christ alone belongs "the glory and the dominion." He alone has the right to rule.

Consequently, Christ's final call is a *sovereign call*. It comes down from heaven's throne to the church, with authority over every other human voice that calls for our attention and allegiance.

AN URGENT CALL

This final call is urgent. Time is short. The end of this age approaches. Christ's coming is soon. In fact, Christ is already in the process of coming. So, we must answer His call *now!*

> Behold, He is coming with the clouds, and every eye will see Him, even those who pierced Him; and all the tribes of the earth will mourn over Him. Even so. Amen (Revelation 1:7).

The curtain is ready to fall with finality on the theater of human history. The unfolding drama of redemption is all but complete. All that remains is the climactic return of our Lord. This final call comes with urgency because the Lord is coming back soon. So, we must answer His call *now!*

The above passage does not say, "He *will* come." Rather, it says, "He *is* coming"—present tense. His coming is so imminent that He is already in the process of coming.

"The time is *near*" (Revelation 1:3). This means that the time is brief. Opportunity is short. His coming is *here!* The time for action is upon us. Today is the most important time in all human history. These are the moments immediately preceding the return of Jesus Christ.

When Christ does appear, His coming will be in great glory. He will be attended by the clouds, which picture all the saints dressed in white robes who accompany His return (Revelation 19:8, 14). They are the "cloud of witnesses" (Hebrews 12:1) now in heaven. There are so many believers returning with Christ at His coming that they appear visually to be massive clouds rolling across the skies.

Every eye will see Him. In that day, His glory will not be veiled. This time, there will be no mistaking His identity. At His first coming, Christ's glory was veiled by human flesh. But at His second coming, "they will see the Son of Man coming on the clouds of the sky with power and great glory" (Matthew 24:30).

Because Christ's coming is so imminent, His final call creates a sense of urgency in our hearts. *Now* is the time to wake up and serve Him!

A couple retired to bed for the evening. As they laid their heads on their pillows, the grandfather clock downstairs began to chime.

Ten o'clock! Eleven o'clock! Twelve o'clock!

But it continued to sound.

Thirteen o'clock! Fourteen o'clock! Fifteen o'clock!

Hearing all *fifteen* chimes, the husband popped his head up in startled amazement. His wife rolled over and asked him, "Honey, what time is it?"

"I don't know," he replied, "but it's later than it's ever been before."

That's true about Christ's return. None of us knows the hour He is coming. But it's later than it's ever been before.

Yet, the church sleeps. Comfortably tucked in bed. Late into the night. We live as if we don't know what time it is. We conduct our business as if His coming is a long time off. But the time is *near!*

Paul writes, "It is already the hour for you to awaken from sleep; for now salvation is nearer to us than when we believed. The night is almost gone, and the day is at hand" (Romans 13:11-12). This pictures someone asleep in the early-morning hours. It's still dark, just before the first streaks of dawn break across the eastern horizon. It's time to wake up and get with it. The dawn of Christ's return is ready to break. At any moment. We must wake up now.

Look *who* is coming!

> *"I am the Alpha and the Omega," says the Lord God, "who is and who was and who is to come, the Almighty" (Revelation 1:8).*

Alpha and *omega* are the first and last letters of the Greek alphabet. The beginning and the end! All letters find their place between these two. "The Alpha and the Omega" encompass the whole. No letter precedes *alpha*. No letter comes after *omega*.

When Jesus says, "I am the Alpha and the Omega," He is making a claim to Deity. From A to Z, He is the beginning and the end, the One who encompasses the whole of creation. Nothing comes before Him. No one will come after Him. "For from Him and through Him and to Him are all things " (Romans 11:36).

Jesus Christ, the Lord God, is the One who "was," "is," and "is to come." He is eternally the same—past, present, and future. Unchanging. Immutable. Never diminishing in His power. Ever the same yesterday, today, and forever (Hebrews 13:8).

As the Lord God who "is to come," Jesus is the One who is about to arrive. Later in the book of Revelation, when the time finally comes for Jesus to come, He is described as the "Lord God, the Almighty, who art and who wast" (11:17). But "who is to come" is omitted there. Why?

Because the time of Christ's appearing will no longer be anticipatory. The time of His coming will be finally realized in that day.

But today, He is the One who "is to come." He is about to arrive. Very quickly. Soon. So, we must answer His call *now*.

Christ is also "the Almighty"—the One possessing all power. Again, this is another staggering claim for Deity. This title is used only of God and Christ. Never of a man. There is no power in the universe outside of Christ. There is nothing He cannot do, because there are no boundaries to His power.

The hour is late in America. Night has come to the world. Darkness is draped across the land. Jesus is soon to come as "a thief in the night" (1 Thessalonians 5:2). The church must be ready.

It's midnight again.

AN UNEXPECTED CALL

Just when the hour seemed the darkest, the call came. The year is A.D. 95. The scene is a lonely island in the Mediterranean Sea—the island of Patmos.

Patmos was a barren, desolate, rocky island off the coast of Asia Minor. Hardly a tourist trap for retired apostles. It was here that one man—John—was chosen to receive the final call.

> *I, John, your brother and fellow-partaker in the tribulation and kingdom and perseverance which are in Jesus, was on the island called Patmos, because of the word of God and the testimony of Jesus (Revelation 1:9).*

This is John, the brother of James. A Son of Zebedee. One of the "sons of thunder." A fisherman from Galilee. One of the twelve disciples. The author of one of the Gospels. The author of three epistles. The last living apostle. The leader of the Asian churches.

When the call came, the aged apostle was in exile on Patmos, suffering for his faith in Christ. The island is one of about fifty small islands called the Dodecanese. It is about ten miles long and five miles wide. Thin and narrow, this island is shaped like a crescent with an open harbor facing east—a safe place for vessels to tie up in during storms. But it was no safe place for humans. Not in the first century. Patmos was a penal colony, settled by the Romans. It was the Alcatraz of the day. Like being shipped to Siberia for the winter. It was a remote place of exile for serious criminals against the Empire.

If the crime was political, the prisoner would have limited freedom to move about on the island. But if the crime was religious or criminal, the condemned man was enslaved to hard labor as part of a chain gang. John was surely suffering the latter because of his faith in Jesus Christ.

So, the apostle is laboring in the mines and quarries of Patmos. Busting rocks on a chain gang. Ninety years old. Separated from believers. Suffering persecution for Christ. Aged and forgotten. Confined.

He is without sufficient food. Improperly dressed. Sleeping on the bare ground of a dark cave. Cold. Lonely. Under the severe lash of an overseer. Imprisoned for the criminal offense of preaching the gospel of Jesus Christ.

John identifies himself to the church as "your brother and fellow-partaker in the tribulation and kingdom and perseverance which are in Jesus." Simply a brother in Christ and a fellow-sufferer. Not an apostle. Not the leader of the churches. Why such a non-apostolic identification here? Because at the moment, it seems that the days of his apostolic ministry are behind him. John seems to be abandoned to this island to serve out the remaining days of his life.

John is suffering this persecution because of his faith in Christ. Years earlier, Nero had launched a great attack against the church. In his maddening rule, he lit his arenas with Christian bodies in a violent persecution of the early church. But this emperor soon died, and there was a temporary lull in the storm. Then Domitian took the throne, and he came with a fury worse than Nero's.

It is under Domitian that John and the church are now suffering in an unprecedented, empire-wide persecution of Christians.

He instigated emperor worship as an imperial cult to hold together the expanding Roman Empire. It became law that no Christian escape punishment who failed to worship Caesar and to renounce his allegiance to Jesus Christ.

John refused to recant his faith in Christ. When brought before the tribunal, he would not deny his Lord. His perseverance in the faith was unwavering. So, he was sentenced to confinement on Patmos for his refusal to worship the emperor.

It is when we are suffering and forgotten that God often unexpectedly breaks into our lives to use us in the greatest ways. This was true of John. And it is often true for us. John thought that his life and long ministry were over, but his most significant ministry was still before him. Similarly, your most significant ministry may be right around the corner as well.

Over half a century earlier, Christ had commissioned the church to reach the world with the gospel. John and the early church obeyed, making initial inroads into Asia Minor and Europe. But in sixty years the cause of Christianity had hardly made a dent in the mighty Roman Empire. Rather than converting the world, the world had, seemingly, conquered the church. The believers are scattered throughout Asia Minor, huddled in fear for their lives.

Hardly a world movement.

Jesus had promised to be with them to the end of the age (Matthew 28:20). But now John is exiled, and the church appears to be an endangered species. Has Christ abandoned them? Where is God?

What's gone wrong?

It was at this time—when the church was suffering the most and was seemingly defeated—that Christ broke into John's life and issued His final call. When the hour was the darkest—that was precisely when God sounded His call.

It is the same today. It is now, when America seems to be entering her darkest hour, that this call must ring out the loudest. It is now, when our government and culture are sinking into greater godlessness, that this final call must be heard.

A COMPELLING CALL

It was in the midst of imprisonment that John heard the final call of Jesus Christ.

> *I was in the Spirit on the Lord's day, and I heard behind me a loud voice like the sound of a trumpet (Revelation 1:10).*

Unexpectedly—while suffering on Patmos—John is overpowered by the Holy Spirit. The apostle is catapulted by the Holy Spirit into the unseen spiritual world. It's hard to describe exactly what happened. Paul had a similar experience, and even he didn't know if he was in his body or out of it (2 Corinthians 12:1-4). Dramatically, John transcends above and beyond his normal human apprehension. He is supernaturally elevated beyond his natural senses to a higher spiritual level to receive direct revelation from God.

It is in this state of spiritual ecstasy that John hears a voice. A voice like a mighty *trumpet call*. It is piercing. Authoritative. Militant. Commanding. Compelling. Arresting. Brilliant. Shrill.

This trumpet-like voice is the voice of *Jesus Christ!*

It has been over 65 years since John last heard this familiar voice. Six decades earlier, John heard this voice call him to leave his nets to follow Him. More than half a century ago, he heard this voice cry out from the cross, "It is finished!"

Now John hears that voice again!

Only this time, it's different. John doesn't hear the gentle whisper of the Lord's Servant. The prophet said, "He will not cry out or raise His voice, nor make His voice heard in the street" (Isaiah 42:2). Instead, he hears the loud, piercing voice of the glorified Christ. Like a mighty trumpet blast!

When John hears it, he, no doubt, almost jumps out of his skin! His heart stops. His hair stands up. His head jerks.

The trumpet-like simile is significant. Throughout the pages of Scripture, the trumpet is an instrument of power. The trumpets of that day were made from rams' horns. In fact, the word for "trumpet" (*shophar*) derives its name from the horn of a ram that he used to butt and overpower his enemies.

Trumpets were used for various purposes in Scripture. But in each case, the strong blast of the trumpet signaled something powerful and compelling.

First, the trumpet was used *to signal the presence of God*. It signified to God's people that God was near, causing them to tremble (Exodus 19:16; 20:18). The sound of the trumpet announced the very voice of God (Exodus 19:19). Similarly, it provided the assurance of His presence as the defender of His people (Nehemiah 4:20). At the Rapture, the trumpet blast will signal the appearance of God—Jesus Christ—in the sky to take His church home (1 Thessalonians 4:16).

Second, the trumpet was used *to call God's people to action or to battle*. The sounding of the trumpet frequently was a signal to God's people to move forward into action. It was used to lead the charge into battle (Joshua 6:20), to summon the people (Judges 6:34), to prepare for battle (Judges 7:8), to cease fighting (2 Samuel 2:28; 18:16), to disperse the people (2 Samuel 20:22), and to gather them together (Jeremiah 4:5).

Third, the trumpet was used *to call God's people to worship*. In the book of Leviticus, the sounding of the trumpet was used to commemorate a sacred assembly of God's people (23:24) and to signify the importance of the Day of Atonement (25:9). In Revelation 4:1, John is caught up to heaven with a voice like a trumpet to behold and worship God's majesty.

Finally, the trumpet was used *to signal the impending judgment of God*. It was used to warn people of impending wrath (Ezekiel 7:14; 33:3, 5). In the Great Tribulation, seven trumpets will be sounded by seven angels to pronounce God's wrath on the world (Revelation 8:7, 8, 10, 12; 9:1, 13; 11:15).

The trumpet was a compelling wake-up call to God's people. Riveting. Commanding. It signaled God's presence. It was a call to war and to worship. And it warned of approaching judgment. That's precisely what this trumpet-like voice of Christ signaled to John. It signaled the awesome presence of God—Jesus Christ (Revelation 1:12-17). It sounded a call to worship Him (Revelation 1:17-20). It sounded a call to action and warned of judgment (Revelation 2—3).

Only this same trumpet call—*the final call*—can awaken the slumbering church today. The trumpet voice of Christ must resound again today. The sleeping church must wake up and answer her Lord's call to arms! She must jump to her feet! She must prepare for the battle at hand! The hour is late! The night is dark! The times are desperate!

Awaken, slumbering church!

A TIMELESS CALL

This final call echoes down through the centuries to the church today. It is still being sounded. It comes down from the first century to the present day.

"Write in a book what you see, and send it to the seven churches: to
Ephesus and to Smyrna and to Pergamum and to Thyatira and to Sardis
and to Philadelphia and to Laodicea" (Revelation 1:11).

John is told to write down what he sees. This call is to be permanently recorded in the inspired canon of Scripture. Christ now
commissions John to write in a book—the book of Revelation—
what is His final call. This call addresses every church and every
believer from the first century until Christ returns.

Why send Christ's message to the *churches*? Why not to the
Roman Empire? Why not send it to the Emperor Domitian and
"straighten out the mess" in the government?

Because God's work on earth is accomplished primarily through
His churches. Instead of sending a letter to Caesar to clean up the
government, God's chief focus was to revive His churches, who, in
turn, would be His light and salt in the world. When the church
becomes vibrant in its faith, then—and only then—will its spiritual
influence be felt in the nation.

Many people today want to make our government the target of
their ministry efforts, in an attempt to save the country. That is a mis-
directed focus. It is the *church* that God wants to use to change
America. True change can only come from within. And only God
working through the church can change hearts in America. So, the
church—not the government—is God's primary agent for change in
the nation.

America can be no stronger than the spiritual life of our
churches. The Bible says, "Righteousness exalts a nation, but sin is
a disgrace to any people" (Proverbs 14:34). The greatness of any
nation lies in her righteousness. And a nation's righteousness is
dependent upon the spiritual life of her churches.

When our nation was very young, the famous French political
philosopher Alexis de Tocqueville visited America. His mission was
to learn what quality enabled a handful of people to defeat the
mighty British Empire. Here was his discovery:

I sought for the greatness and genius of America in her com-
modious harbors and her ample rivers, and it was not there; in
the fertile fields and the boundless prairies, and it was not there;

> in her rich mines and her vast world commerce, and it was not there. Not until I went into the churches of America, and heard her pulpits aflame with righteousness, did I understand the secrets of her genius and power. America is great because she is good, and if America ever ceases to be good, America will cease to be great.

America is in grave danger of losing her goodness. And with it, losing her greatness. Darkness blankets the land. The light of the church is becoming weaker.

It's midnight again.

So, we are not surprised that Jesus Christ addresses the churches in Asia Minor —and not the emperor in Rome. The key to changing the world is revival in the church, not fixing the government.

These churches—Ephesus, Smyrna, Pergamum, Thyatira, Sardis, Philadelphia, and Laodicea—are located in seven cities. Why *these* seven?

Certainly, these were not the most prominent churches of that day. Only two of these seven were even mentioned previously in the Bible—Ephesus and Laodicea. Our Lord might have selected the church at Jerusalem, Antioch, Corinth, Rome, Colossae, Alexandria, or Hierapolis.

Why *these* seven?

These churches were chosen because they were representative assemblies with regard to their spiritual condition. What Christ will say to them will speak to all types of churches in the first and every subsequent century. Also, these seven churches were very likely the ones with whom John had enjoyed the closest relationship. It is quite probable that those seven churches from Asia Minor, where John had served nearly thirty years, sent messengers to assist him in his exile.

These seven cities were all situated on a circular road that networked them together. It was along this road that a postal worker would travel in delivering mail to these seven cities.

On the island of Patmos, John gave the scroll of Revelation to these seven messengers, who crossed the Aegean Sea and found their way to Ephesus. Upon arrival in Ephesus, the messenger would present the scroll to the pastor of the church—unless the messenger was the pastor himself—who would read it publicly to the congregation (Revelation 1:3). He would make a copy before the other messengers would depart with the original document to the next city (compare 22:18-19). Thus, all seven churches received the entirety of the book of Revelation.

Starting from Ephesus and moving clockwise, the other six messengers would have traveled northward about 40 miles to Smyrna. Then the remaining five messengers would journey the 40 miles to Pergamum. Next the other four would move in a southeasterly direction some 45 miles to Thyatira. Then the remaining three proceeded about 30 miles south to Sardis. Then the last two traveled 30 miles east-southeast to Philadelphia. Finally, one messenger would journey 40 miles southeast to Laodicea. To use the visual aid of a clock, this route would complete a half-circle from Ephesus, at 8 o'clock, to Laodicea, at 4 o'clock.

Like Paul Revere sounding his alarm through the New England countryside, these seven messengers dispatched the final call throughout Asia Minor.

Every experience in John's life was preparatory for this one assignment. All the years of instruction from Christ. All the decades of preaching Christ. All the years of leading His churches. All the months of writing sacred Scripture. All these experiences had uniquely prepared John for this one monumental task—dispatching the final call.

And it was all so unexpected. God used John at the *most unexpected time*—while in his nineties. In the *most unlikely place*—while exiled on Patmos. During the *most severe trial*—while a political prisoner of Rome. In the *most unusual way*—while "in the Spirit on the Lord's Day." To fulfill the *most incredible ministry*—to write the book of Revelation.

This call, permanently recorded by John in Scripture, comes down to the church today. Unalterable. Unchanging. Enduring. Permanent. Christ is *still* calling to His church. Just as sovereignly, urgently, and arrestingly as He did when He first issued this call.

This final call must be sounded until Christ comes back. Then will we hear Christ's own audible voice when "the Lord Himself will descend from heaven with a shout" (1 Thessalonians 4:16).

This book is the resounding of Christ's final call. I want to—no, I must—blow this trumpet and sound Christ's call. Why?

It's midnight in America again.

And, once more, *the call* must go out.

A shroud of darkness covers America. While the future of our nation hangs precariously in the balance, the church sleeps. Content to slumber and lie comfortably tucked in bed. Content to pull the covers up over her head.

But the war wages on.

The struggle for the soul of America escalates. The battle for the heart of our nation builds. And only the *church* can stem the tide of darkness. Only the *church* can repel the forces of evil. Let the church be the church!

Whatever became of Paul Revere?

After the Revolutionary War, America's first hero went on to become a noted silversmith in the young nation he helped birth. He set up a foundry to cast church bells. Revere made 398 bells, most of them weighing at least 500 pounds each. Seventy-five of these bells *still* ring in New England steeples. To this day, the legacy of Paul Revere yet rings throughout America.

Like Paul Revere's famous ride, this book is a midnight ride through the churches of America. The call must ring out again across the land. From the pulpits and pews of every church in America, our Lord's final call must be sounded. It must go out far and wide.

A new generation of Minutemen must answer the call. A new army of believers must rally the minute they hear Christ's call. Covers must be thrown off. Candles must be lit. Curtains thrown back. Muskets grabbed. And shots fired into the night.

This call must be sounded throughout America today.

Loudly.

Clearly.

Urgently.

The call must go out.

II

THE AWESOME VISION

Revelation 1:12–16

WE ARE FACING A CRISIS IN AMERICA TODAY. A crisis of epidemic proportions. At its heart, this gathering storm is a crisis of authority.

Almost every form of God-ordained authority is now teetering and on the verge of collapse. The foundations of our American society are cracked and crumbling beneath us. Across the land, all divinely established authority is being challenged.

John Stott writes, "Seldom if ever in its long history has the world witnessed such a self-conscious revolt against authority. All the accepted authorities are being challenged. Anything which savors of establishment is being scrutinized and opposed."

God's authority within *the family* is under siege. Passive men have abandoned their God-assigned leadership in the home, forfeiting their role of headship. Radical feminism is assaulting the traditional role of women, ridiculing God's design of submission. Parental authority is being eroded by a godless culture which is raising a generation of undisciplined children.

God's authority within *the state* is being attacked. Rap songs shout hatred toward police officers in blue uniforms. Embittered communities riot in the streets to protest unpopular court decisions.

God's authority within *the workplace* is being assailed. Labor unions strike against management and form picket lines if their every demand is not quickly met. Terminated employees are suing their bosses even when justly fired.

God's authority within *the classroom* is being threatened. Unruly students are harassing their teachers, even threatening their lives. Discontent schoolteachers are striking against their school boards. The Ten Commandments and prayer have been outlawed from the classroom.

But, most tragic, the crisis rages in *the church*.

Even God's authority with the church is under attack. Martyn Lloyd-Jones writes, "The source of confusion about authority lies in the church itself. Things are as they are in the world today because the church has abandoned its authority."

Seminaries, pastors, and even entire denominations are abandoning the authority of God's Word. The inspired Scriptures are fast becoming the feeble opinions and mythical stories of an ancient, outdated book. Even many Bible-believing churches are holding to their traditions and man-made documents with greater fervor than they do the authority of Scripture.

Moreover, the authority of pastoral leadership is being overturned. Congregations are no longer following their spiritual leaders but are deputizing their own posses and are forming their own lynching mobs to take the law into their own hands.

But most of all, *the Lordship of Jesus Christ* is being assailed by the church. Recognizing His sovereign Lordship is considered optional by many church movements now as it relates to salvation and sanctification.

At the core of this entire crisis—whether it be in the family, the state, the workplace, the school, or the church—is the issue of submission to divinely established authority. If society and the church are to function properly, every aspect must be brought, ultimately, into submission to God-ordained authority.

Enthroned at the right hand of God, Jesus Christ alone possesses all authority. Jesus said, "All authority has been given to Me in heaven and on earth" (Matthew 28:18). He alone is unaccountable. He alone has no one over Him. Thus, He alone has the right to speak and act as He pleases. All creation is under Him. Every human institution receives its authority, in one way or another, from His sovereign authority (John 19:11).

The need of the hour is this: we must regain our vision of the sovereign authority of Jesus Christ. And this must begin in the church. We must see Him as He is—enthroned, exalted, sovereign, ruling, and reigning—and then be brought into humble submission to His Lordship. Then, and only then, will we experience a spiritual awakening in the church that will spread, like a raging prairie fire, across the land.

In the last chapter, we observed John exiled to the island of Patmos because of his faith in Jesus Christ. An aged man, probably in his nineties, John was the last living apostle. The year is A.D. 95. While imprisoned on Patmos, John was unexpectedly overcome by the Holy Spirit and heard a loud voice like a trumpet speaking.

The voice was none other than Jesus Christ! John was told to record Christ's final call to His church. He was instructed to write in a book what he saw and heard and send it to seven churches in Asia Minor.

But before John is told *what* to write to the churches, he is shown *who* is the Head of the church. The church must first see Christ's sovereign Lordship before she hears what He says. Our conscience must first be bound to obeying Him.

As John turns to the voice, he sees the awesome vision of Jesus Christ. Not Jesus as He once *was*—in the form of a lowly bond-servant. But Christ as He *is*—the King of kings and Lord of lords. John beholds the overwhelming glory of Jesus Christ!

> *And I turned to see the voice that was speaking with me. And having turned I saw seven golden lampstands; and in the middle of the lampstands one like a son of man, clothed in a robe reaching to the feet, and girded across His breasts with a golden girdle. And His head and His hair were white like white wool, like snow; and His eyes were like a flame of fire; and His feet were like burnished bronze, when it has been caused to glow in a furnace, and His voice was like the sound of many waters. And in His right hand He held seven stars; and out of His mouth came a sharp two-edged sword; and His face was like the sun shining in its strength (Revelation 1:12-16).*

This vision of Christ—awesome, majestic, transcendent—reveals Christ's glory with great and striking detail. Because human language fails John, he struggles to communicate this awesome vision. So, he must employ vivid imagery to record the vision for us. May God now open our eyes to behold the glorified Christ.

HIS SUPREME PRESENCE

The first feature that captures John's attention is Christ's position. He is standing in the midst of His churches. He is occupying the place of supreme preeminence among the churches—moving about freely among them.

> And I turned to see the voice that was speaking with me. And having turned I saw seven golden lampstands; and in the middle of the lampstands, one like a son of man (Revelation 1:12-13a).

As John hears the trumpet-like voice, he turns and first sees seven golden lampstands. In ancient times, a lampstand was put in the corner of a room, and a small oil lamp was set atop it. The purpose of the lampstand was, quite simply, to hold the lamp aloft most prominently in the room. The lampstand was not the light itself. It was to bear the light.

These seven lampstands are, clearly, the seven churches (Revelation 1:20). We are to bear the light of Jesus Christ to a dark world. This is the purpose of the church.

These lampstands are seven in number. The number *seven* represents fullness or completion. These lampstands represent seven literal churches in Asia Minor, but they also symbolize *all* churches down through the ages. What Jesus says to these churches will speak to all churches and all believers in all times.

These lampstands are made of gold. Gold is the most costly precious metal. It is of greatest value. Gold represents the great value of the church to Christ. If market value is determined by what someone is willing to pay for an item, then our value is inestimable. Jesus shed His priceless blood to purchase the church, a fortune far greater than gold or silver (1 Peter 1:18-19). We are precious to Him!

Incredibly, in the midst of the lampstands, John sees a human-like figure. This is no ordinary human, but someone "like a son of man." "Son of Man" is a Messianic title deeply rooted in the Old

Testament that speaks of the One who would come, anointed by God's Spirit, to inaugurate God's kingdom on the earth.

The prophet Daniel saw the Son of Man coming to rule the world with sovereign authority. "I kept looking in the night visions, and behold, with the clouds of heaven, *one like a Son of Man was coming*. . . . And to Him was given dominion, glory and a kingdom, that all the peoples, nations, and men of every language might serve Him. His dominion is an everlasting dominion which will not pass away; and His kingdom is one which will not be destroyed" (Daniel 7:13-14).

The Son of *Man* is Jesus Christ—the Son of *God*. He is as completely God as if he were not man. And He is as completely man as if He were not God. Not half God, half man. But perfectly God, perfectly man. The *God-man!*

Jesus is the Lord of the whole universe. He possesses absolute authority over all the world. No part of creation lies outside His Lordship. This is especially true in His church. Jesus is the supreme Sovereign over each congregation. The Head of each church body. The Chief Cornerstone of each local assembly. Everything must be brought into alignment with Him.

Ultimately, no church is to be run by any man, leadership team, or special interest group. Nor is it to be run by charter members, the congregation, or denominational headquarters. Jesus *alone* walks in the midst of the lampstands. And He *alone* is to rule His church.

How much awareness is there in our churches today of His right to rule? How many church board meetings are run with this solemn awareness? How many worship services are participated in with this sobering realization?

Jesus still stands at the center of His church. He is the hub, and every spoke in the church must intersect in Him. He is in the place of absolute supremacy and centrality in His church. This precious truth should govern and control our thoughts, our words, and our behavior any time we come together as the church—be it for worship, for fellowship, or for ministry.

HIS SOVEREIGN ATTIRE

The next feature that John notices is the distinguished dress of Christ. He is seen clothed in regal garb, again signifying His sovereign authority over the church. Jesus is wearing the vestments of the One in control.

> *. . . clothed in a robe reaching to the feet, and girded across the breasts with a golden girdle (Revelation 1:13b).*

John continues to look and sees Christ wearing a long robe, draped with a golden sash. In ancient times, this was the recognized apparel of authority, dignity, and rulership. The longer the robe, the greater was one's authority. Thus, in Isaiah's vision of the glorified Christ, the train of His robe filled the temple (Isaiah 6:1), signifying the boundless dominion of Christ that could not be contained by the temple.

In Old Testament times, a long robe was the attire of spiritual leaders of high rank, whether it be the high priest (Exodus 25, 28, 29, 35; Zechariah 3:4), a king (1 Samuel 24:5, 11), a prince (Ezekiel 26:16), or a judge (Ezekiel 9:1-11). Such a stately robe hung down to the feet, setting him apart as the one who ruled for God. Whether it was worn by a king, judge, prince, priest, or prophet, this attire adorned the man who ruled on God's behalf.

Jesus is all these—Prophet, Priest, and King to His churches, as well as Judge. As Prophet, He speaks for God to the people. As High Priest, He intercedes for the people before God. As King, He rules over the people for God. As Judge, He presides and deliberates over the people. All these images are represented here.

This is how John sees Christ. Wearing sovereign attire. Bearing the garments of regal majesty. Adorned with absolute authority. His verdicts are undisputed. His authority is unlimited. His reign is unrivaled.

Jesus alone has the right to control His churches. He calls its pastors. He adds to its membership. He causes its growth. He blesses its ministries. He purifies its membership. He expands its influence. He provides for its needs. And He overturns its enemies.

"I will build My church; and the gates of Hades shall not overpower it" (Matthew 16:18). He is the Builder; we are His instruments.

HIS SINLESS CHARACTER

From His clothing, John's focus looks upward to behold Christ's head and hair.

And His head and His hair were white like white wool, like snow (Revelation 1:14a).

Jesus' head and hair is pure white. It is a blazing white that shines as brilliantly as freshly fallen snow on a sunlit day. The reflection is blinding. This dazzling white is a symbol of Christ's absolute sinless holiness (Daniel 7:9). Holiness is the most prominent of all Christ's attributes. The crown of His attributes. Appropriately, His holiness sits atop His divine head, the place where a king's regal crown would rest.

Holiness means *separateness*. It comes from a Semitic root that means "to cut." Something would be cut in half and the two parts separated. It means that Christ is separated from all mankind. He is a cut above us. High and lifted up. Lofty. Exalted. Majestic. Transcendent. Unlike us. Totally other than us. Infinitely perfect and pure.

Jesus doesn't conform to any standard. He *is* the standard. Because He is holy, He never does anything wrong. He never errs. He never does something that isn't right.

Christ is perfectly holy. His words are *holy*. His judgments are *holy*. His decrees are *holy*. He is *wholly, wholly holy!*

The Bible claims that Jesus "knew *no sin*" (2 Corinthians 5:21). He "has been tempted in all things as we are, yet *without sin*" (Hebrews 4:15). He is *"holy, innocent, undefiled,* separated from sinners" (Hebrews 7:26). He "committed *no sin*, nor was any deceit found in His mouth" (1 Peter 2:22). He is "the *Holy and Righteous One*" (Acts 3:14), "the *Holy One* of God" (Luke 4:34), in whom "there is *no sin*" (1 John 3:5).

Christ's holiness is seen in His hatred of sin. He is totally removed from it. To be in His presence, one must be holy. When the angels sinned, they were immediately cast out of heaven and separated from His presence. Why? Because He is holy. When men reject Christ today, they ultimately will be cast away from His presence. Only faith in Christ, resulting in the imputation of Christ's own holiness to us, makes us fit for heaven.

It is holiness that Christ requires of His church. We must be separated from the world—different—not like the world.

Peter wrote, "Like the Holy One who called you, be holy yourselves also in all your behavior, because it is written, 'You shall be holy, for I am holy'" (1 Peter 1:15-16).

Despite the degenerating morals of the day, Jesus has not lowered His standard one iota. The church must be a pure bride, without spot or blemish. A chaste virgin. Not flirting with the world. Holy. Innocent. Undefiled. Rather than becoming like the world, she must remain holy. Holiness is what distinguishes us from the world.

We must *be different* if we are to *make a difference*.

HIS SEARCHING GAZE

While peering at Christ's head, John notices His eyes. The divine vision now becomes even more terrifying. John sees Christ with fiery lasers flashing out of each eye socket!

And His eyes were like a flame of fire (Revelation 1:14b).

Flaming searchlights are shining out of each eye. He sees with a penetrating, piercing gaze. He sees into the depths and secret places of every church. Nothing is hidden! "There is no creature hidden from His sight, but all things are open and laid bare to the eyes of Him with whom we have to do" (Hebrews 4:13).

With holy intelligence, Jesus knows every detail about every member in every church. Nothing escapes His attention. He never has to gather information or ask questions. He never learns anything. Who would teach Him? He sees every minister, notes every member, observes every ministry, and views every motive perfectly with X-ray vision.

A. W. Tozer writes, "Because God knows all things perfectly, He knows no thing better than any other thing, but all things equally well. He never discovers anything. He is never surprised, never amazed."

Matthew Henry wrote, "God not only sees men, he sees *through* them."

There is no place to hide. Nothing can obscure His vision. No knowledge is out of His reach. With blazing insight and penetrating gaze, He fully knows every detail about us. Even the darkness is not dark to Him (Psalm 139:12). The very hairs of our head are numbered (Luke 12:7). Not even a sparrow escapes His notice.

How much more must He know our minds (Luke 6:8) and hearts (John 2:25). There isn't a secret thought, word, or deed hidden from Christ. In fact, He knows our thoughts before we can even express them (Psalm 139:4). He reads our mail without ever opening the envelope.

With eyes aflame, Jesus is looking in His churches for holiness! With searching gaze, He says to the church at Ephesus, "I *know* your deeds" (2:2). To Smyrna He says, "I *know* your tribulation" (2:9). To Pergamum, "I *know* where you dwell" (2:13). Likewise, to the churches at Thyatira, Sardis, Philadelphia, and Laodicea, "I *know* your deeds" (2:19; 3:1, 8, 15). He knows it all!

Christ is *inescapable*. There is no place we can hide from Him. What is it that Jesus is looking for?

Holiness.

HIS SMOLDERING JUDGMENT

From His fiery eyes, John now looks downward to Jesus' red-hot feet. The aged apostle discovers that Christ's feet are glowing like burnished metal in a fiery furnace.

> *And His feet were like burnished bronze, when it has been caused to glow in a furnace (Revelation 1:15a).*

Here is pictured Christ's righteous judgment against sin. Because Jesus is holy, He cannot tolerate sin. He loves righteousness but loathes sin. Even in the church?

Especially in the church!

Do you hate weeds more in your neighbor's yard or in your own? Of course, you hate them *especially* in your own yard! Do you hate cancer more in your neighbor's family or in your own family? You hate to see it in any family but *especially* in your own. In the same way, Christ *especially* hates sin in His own spiritual family. More so than in the world.

Consider Christ's cleansing of the temple. There, he displayed His holy anger against sin. When he saw the hypocrisy within His Father's house, He made a whip, overturned the tables, and drove out the hypocrisy. With holy zeal, Jesus judged the sin in His Father's house of worship. God's name was being dishonored!

So today, Jesus responds with holy rage against sin in the

churches. Because He is omniscient, He sees into every church perfectly. Because He is holy, He reacts against sin among His own people. Because He is righteous, He must judge sin in the church.

Unfortunately, most people—even many well-meaning
Christians—have an aversion toward Jesus as a God of judgment.
Especially in the church. Yet, Scripture clearly paints a fearful and ter-
rifying picture of His righteous anger against sin in the church (Acts
5:1-11). Today churches are soft-pedaling this severe truth about
Christ's judgment. Some pastors have quietly omitted it.
Nevertheless, Christ is a consuming fire who judges His people (1
Corinthians 3:13-15). Some of the Hebrew words used in the Bible
reveal Christ's fiery judgment of our sin. One word (*charah*) means "to
become heated up, to burn with fury." God's anger was kindled against
His own people because of their immorality (Numbers 25:3). Another
word (*charon*) refers to a burning, fierce wrath. God's anger burned
against His people because they turned to idolatry (Exodus 32:12).

With feet aflame, Jesus stands before His church. His white-hot
anger is kindled against sin. Burning with displeasure, His wrath is
torched against our sin. As our Holy Judge, He *must* judge sin in the
church.

This picture—His divine feet like burnished bronze, glowing in
a furnace—is drawn from the world of metal refining. In ancient
times, precious metals were refined in massive furnaces that were
glowing red-hot. The heat was unbearable. The sight terrifying. For
the purification process to occur, the furnace temperatures were
greatly raised. The intensely high temperatures, along with the refining additives, created a volcanic and violent reaction. The foundations of the furnaces began to shake and vibrate. A rumbling and
rocking occurred. As the impure slag rose to the top, it was skimmed
off. Only a pure metal was left behind. The metal was so blinding
that one could not look upon it with the naked eye.

Polished bronze is quite shiny, reflecting all available light. The
pure brass was put in a hot furnace that was raised to the melting
point. The metal was now glowing. The brightness even more blinding. The polished surface of the bronze, in addition to the glowing
metal at extremely high temperatures, multiplied the blinding effect.

The intense heat is felt all around you. The foundations of the furnace are shaking. The sound of the glowing metal is roaring. The sight of white metal is blinding.

This is what John sees! He sees Jesus Christ with feet like burnished bronze, caused to glow in a furnace. The sight is blinding. Terrifying. Intimidating.

Brass, in the Bible, symbolizes judgment. In the tabernacle, the furniture that was associated with the sin offering was made of brass. The fires that burned on the brass altar represented the burning anger of God against sin. Likewise, when Moses lifted up a brass serpent in the wilderness, it was a foreshadowing of the cross where Jesus would become sin under judgment for us (John 3:14-15).

Here, Jesus' brass feet picture that He is standing strong in judgment over our sins. He will judge sin wherever He finds it. He is constantly weighing our churches, measuring our ministries, and auditing our actions. He is judging all that is unholy with the fires of His glowing wrath (1 Corinthians 3:12-15). Everything that is unholy yields to the consuming fire.

To Ephesus Jesus says, *"But I have this against you*, that you left your first love" (2:4). To Pergamum He says, *"But I have a few things against you* . . . you have there some who hold the teaching of Balaam . . . [and] the Nicolaitans" (2:14-15). To Thyatira, *"But I have this against you*, that you tolerate the woman Jezebel" (2:20). To Sardis He pronounces, "You are dead" (3:1). And to Laodicea He says, "You are neither cold nor hot . . . you are lukewarm" (3:15-16).

Make no mistake. Jesus will judge sin in His churches. "It is time for judgment to begin with the household of God" (1 Peter 4:17).

Any church is either *on fire* or *in the fire!*

HIS STRONG VOICE

The awesome vision of Christ moves now from *sight* to *sound*. John's focus moves from what he *sees* to what he *hears*. The apostle hears the voice of Christ speaking to His churches, powerfully and authoritatively.

And His voice was like the sound of many waters (Revelation 1:15b).

As Jesus speaks, this is no ordinary voice! He speaks with a voice like mighty ocean waves crashing against the jagged rocks of Patmos.

His voice is like the deafening roar of a powerful waterfall plummeting hundreds of feet below. When Christ speaks, He drowns out all other voices.

I recently stood at the base of Niagara Falls on the Canadian side. The man who drove me there was trying to give me an explanation of the Falls. I say *trying*, because I could not hear a single word he was saying. Not a word.

The roar of millions of gallons of water rushing over the Falls was *deafening!* The cascading waters completely drowned out all that he had to say. I could only hear the roar of the water. Nothing else. And for the next several hours, I could still hear it reverberating in my ears.

So it is with Christ. When He speaks, he utterly drowns out every human voice and man's feeble opinions. What Jesus says to His churches is the final word. His words cannot be refuted. His appraisals cannot be debated. His verdicts cannot be overturned. Nor can His promises be broken.

Because He is holy, Jesus cannot lie (John 14:6). Whatever He says is the absolute truth. He will always have the final word. His Word *is* the final word. Christ speaks to His churches with a voice of thunder. He issues a call to repent.

Jesus says to Ephesus, "Remember therefore from where you have fallen, and *repent*" (2:5). To Pergamum, "Repent therefore; or else . . ." (2:16). To Thyatira He says, "I gave her time to *repent*; and she does not want to *repent*" (2:21). To Sardis, "Remember therefore what you have received and heard; and keep it, and *repent*" (3:3). To Laodicea, "I advise you to buy from Me gold . . . white garments . . . and eyesalve . . . be zealous therefore, and *repent*" (3:18-19).

This is Christ's word to His church—*repent!*

HIS SPIRITUAL LEADERS

How is the voice of Christ heard in the church? *How* does Christ speak to His churches today? *How* can we hear His voice? By the seven stars that Jesus holds in His right hand.

And in His right hand He held seven stars (Revelation 1:16a).

It is through the seven stars that Christ speaks to His churches. They are His mouthpieces through whom His voice is heard.

John identifies these seven stars as "the angels of the seven churches" (Revelation 1:20). Angel (*angelos*) means "a divinely commissioned messenger." One sent from God with a message. Sometimes the messenger is an angelic being. Other times, it is a human being. It all depends upon the context.

Here, these "stars," or angels, refer to human messengers. They picture God-called, Spirit-empowered messengers commissioned by Christ to preach His Word to the churches. These seven angels are the seven pastors, or teaching elders, of the seven churches. There is one messenger for each church who is given the primary responsibility to preach and teach God's Word (2 Timothy 4:1-5).

As the pastor brings God's message, he becomes Christ's mouthpiece to that local assembly. No preacher speaks infallibly or *ex cathedra*. But as long as his message originates from God's Word and squares with sound doctrine, the voice of Christ speaks through him to that congregation. This is how Christ's voice is heard in the church.

The Thessalonian church heard the voice of Christ when Paul, their first pastor, preached to them. The Apostle Paul praised them: "We constantly thank God that when you received from us the word of God's message, you accepted it not as the word of men, but for what it really is, the word of God" (1 Thessalonians 2:13).

Martyn Lloyd-Jones wrote, "What is the chief end of preaching? I think it is this: it is to give men and women a sense of God and His presence." That's it precisely! Pastors are to declare God's message to the church. They are simply delivery boys who bring Christ's message, not the editors who write the story.

Not unexpectedly, Christ holds these men "in His right hand." The place of strictest accountability, special protection, and delegated authority. It is through these men that Christ leads His church. That's why the standard for leadership is so high! Pastors must be spiritually mature men of integrity, humility, and purity who follow God's agenda.

Pray for your pastor. No church can advance beyond the faithful ministry of its leadership.

HIS SEVERE DISCIPLINE

The vision unfolds further. John remains focused upon Christ and notes now that out of His mouth proceeds a deadly weapon—a sword!

And out of His mouth came a sharp, two-edged sword (Revelation 1:16b).

This sharp and two-edged sword portrays Christ's judicial authority to administer discipline in His church. When God's Word is disobeyed, Jesus wields His sword in discipline. This sword (*rhomphaia*) was the large-blade sword used by a warrior in battle against his enemies. While the church is not Christ's enemy, *sin is!*

With this sharp sword, Jesus will surgically remove sin from His body like a life-threatening malignancy! If your body were infected with cancer, you would do everything possible to restore its health. That might require submitting to the surgeon's knife to remove the cancer. Not because you hate your body. But, just the opposite, because you love your body. You would allow the surgeon to cut on you because you want your body to be healthy.

Similarly, because Christ loves His church, He desires its spiritual health. But where He finds sin in the camp, He must painfully cut it out with His two-edged sword and remove it. Not because He hates the church. But because He loves the health of His church.

It is toward *the church* that Jesus draws His sword. This is no idle threat. Either we deal with sin, or He will. But it *will* be dealt with.

To the stale church in Ephesus, He warned that He would remove their ministry, influence, and spiritual power (2:5). To the callous church in Pergamum, He threatened to come and discipline them severely (2:16). To the compromising church in Thyatira, Jesus warned that He would send physical illness, tribulation, and even death (2:22-23). To the carnal church at Sardis, Jesus threatened to remove what spiritual power remained (3:3). To the lukewarm church at Laodicea, He promised to spit them out of His mouth and severely discipline them (3:15-19).

All these actions are pictured in Christ's wielding His sharp, two-edged sword against His churches. Loss of ministry. Painful consequences. War-like casualties. Physical illness. Tribulation. Death. Loss of spiritual power. Forfeit of divine favor. Loss of spiritual blessing.

Maybe you're thinking, "I know of churches that are getting away with their sin." Well, I've often thought that myself. In fact, I have wondered why Christ has let sin go undisciplined in my church. Why *does* God allow sin to go unchecked?

Here's why. In His grace, Christ often withholds His discipline to give us more time to repent. He prefers that *we* deal with the sin. But we must not presume that His delays mean that He won't eventually discipline us. "The Lord is slow to anger and great in power, and the Lord will by no means leave the guilty unpunished" (Nahum 1:3). He is *slow to anger*, but without our repentance, His sword will surely fall against any church that tolerates unholiness.

We don't really understand His holy indignation against sin. We are too easily shocked by His severe reaction against sin.

The real question is not why Christ judges sin so severely. Nor is it why He lets sin go temporarily unpunished. The real question is why He lets *any* of us live. It is only by His grace that we are not consumed.

HIS SHINING SPLENDOR

Here's the final component of the awesome vision. John sees Christ's face shining with the glory of God.

And His face was like the sun shining in its strength (Revelation 1:16c).

John looks into the shining face of Christ and is immediately blinded. This experience is like staring into the burning sun. Here is the radiant glory of His divine countenance. Here is the refulgent glory of God in the face of Christ.

His face shining like the sun is the brilliant display of all that has preceded. It is the shining forth of His sovereignty, holiness, omniscience, and judgment.

The Word *glory* means something that is brilliant, bright, or beautiful. Christ's intrinsic glory is the display of all His divine attributes and essence. It is the sum of what He is. It is the outshining of His divine perfections manifested for all to see. All men have sinned and fall infinitely short of Christ's glory (Romans 3:23).

When Jesus first came into the world, His glory was mostly veiled. He came in the form of a bond-servant, not a King (Philippians 2:6-8). Christ's incarnation, like a lampshade momentarily placed over a brightly burning light, obscured most of His glory. Consequently, most people didn't recognize who He was.

On a few occasions, His glory was clearly revealed. One such occasion was on the Mount of Transfiguration. There, Christ's glory was unveiled, and His face "shone like the sun" (Matthew 17:2). The disciples were in awe. But then God put the lampshade back over Christ's glory, and He returned back into the valley, veiled.

After His death and resurrection, Jesus returned to the right hand of God the Father. There, He returned to the glory that was His before the world began (John 17:5). It is this divine glory that John now beholds. Unveiled. Unmasked. Unadulterated.

So bright is the effulgence of His dazzling glory that in the ages to come there will be no need for the sun. The glory of Christ will illuminate the galaxies! Looking ahead to the eternal state, John writes, "There shall no longer be any night; and they shall not have need of the light of a lamp nor the light of the sun, because the Lord God shall illumine them" (Revelation 22:5). His majestic glory, even brighter than the sun, will light up the whole universe.

What a vision of Christ!

When you close your eyes, is *this* the Christ you see? When you pray, is it *this* Lord before whom you come? When you worship, is *this* the Jesus to whom you sing? When you read your Bible, is it *this* Master you hear?

Let's face it. We have become too casual in our relationship with Christ. Too comfortable. Too horizontal. Too "buddy-buddy"! No wonder a recent survey of ex-church members revealed that the main reason they stopped going to church was that they found it boring.

Boring?

Not *this* Christ!

If a spiritual awakening is to arouse the church, we must first wake up to the glory and holiness of Jesus Christ. Before we can answer His call, we must see again *who* calls.

It is our Sovereign Lord who calls. The One who is above and beyond us. The One who reigns in exalted loftiness. The One who dwells in consuming majesty. The One who reigns in transcendent glory!

This Christ must be worshiped in the church.

And obeyed.

III

HOLY TERROR

Revelation 1:17–20

PEOPLE ARE SCURRYING EVERYWHERE.

The prelude has already begun. Late-arriving worshipers are slipping into their favorite pews. As people are informally chatting, the choir enters the sanctuary and begins their processional march down the side aisles. Up to the front they march, ascending into the choir loft.

Well-dressed deacons are holding the sanctuary doors open and handing out bulletins. As the sunlight is streaming through the stained-glass windows, the beautifully furbished sanctuary is aglow. Ushers are escorting visitors to empty seats. Brightly colored flowers decorate the front altar.

As the prelude builds to a crescendo, the whispering comes to a dramatic halt. It is now time to worship the risen Christ. The organ and piano duet stirs every heart. You can just *feel* it!

The worship pastor discreetly signals with his hand, and the choir rises in perfect unison. With smiles beaming and hearts aglow, they sing the call to worship from the depths of their souls. The anthem invites the spiritually prepared congregation to join them now in offering praise to their great God and Savior.

This is a holy moment.

As if walking onto sacred ground, the pastor moves into the pulpit. With a hand lifted heavenward, he prays and invites the presence of God to fall afresh upon this gathered congregation. The pastor invokes, "God, *come down* out of heaven and visit Your people today. Lord, we *welcome You* in this worship service. *Come now and reveal*

Yourself to us afresh. Fill this service with *the fullness of Your presence*. In Jesus' name, for Your glory, Amen."

Now, suppose—just suppose—God were to *actually* answer that prayer? What if Jesus were to respond to that pastor's request? What if Jesus Himself—bodily, physically, gloriously—actually came to church?

Imagine . . . *Boom!* The back doors of the sanctuary are suddenly flung open. Blinding light floods down the center aisle. The thresholds of the building begin to shake. Pews begin to tremble. Holy smoke begins to pour into the room.

Mysteriously, a Holy Figure moves down the center aisle. The intense heat of His presence is felt, causing all in attendance to swelter and sweat. Wherever this One looks, two laser beams bore holes through the sanctuary walls. He speaks, and the noise is deafening.

There is no mistaking His identity.

The Sovereign Lord of the church—Jesus Christ—has now entered this morning worship service!

The sanctuary has been invaded by the Holy One. Not by the humble carpenter of Nazareth. Nor by the meek teacher from Galilee. But by the gloried Lord of the church. Dressed in regal attire. His head blazing white. His feet glowing like burnished bronze. His voice deafening. Holding seven stars. A sharp sword proceeding out of His mouth. His face shining like the blazing sun. Too bright to even look upon.

Now, let me ask you—what do you think would be the church's response?

How would the worshipers seated in comfortable pews react? How would the choir respond to such a divine visitation? What about the pastor? What would the ushers do?

What would be *your* response?

Would you keep singing? Would you walk over and introduce yourself to Him? Would you invite Him to sit next to you and share a hymnal?

Would you ask Him to explain some mystery that has been perplexing you? Would you run over and hug Him? Would you get Him to sign your Bible?

I doubt it.

The immediate—and only proper—response would be to fall on

your face before Him. We would be blinded by His glory. Covering our faces, we would drop to the ground in humble adoration. No one in the building would remain standing, much less initiate conversation. With fear and trembling, we would acknowledge His divine presence by collapsing to the floor.

This is precisely how the Apostle John responded to the awesome vision of Christ. One Sunday, Jesus Christ Himself suddenly walked into John's worship experience. A voice like a trumpet commanded John's attention. When John turned around, he beheld Christ's awesome glory. Unveiled. Unhindered. Unadulterated.

He fell to the ground like cut timber.

Anything less would have been blasphemy.

Here's the point. Jesus walks among His lampstands and *still* reveals Himself to His people. He *does* come to church. We must respond appropriately to who He is. We would *not* walk over to Christ and shake His hand. *Nor* would we invite Him to sit down next to us and share a hymnal. We *wouldn't* even ask Him some question that we've always wanted to ask Him. Our response would be the same as John's response.

Holy terror would grip our hearts. We would be filled with immediate submission. Conviction. Confession. Adoration. Restoration. Reassurance. And comfort.

Here is John's response to the awesome vision. May his response be ours.

> And when I saw Him, I fell at His feet as a dead man. And He laid His right hand upon me, saying, "Do not be afraid; I am the first and the last, and the living One; and I was dead, and behold, I am alive forevermore, and I have the keys of death and of Hades. Write therefore the things which you have seen, and the things which are, and the things which shall take place after these things. As for the mystery of the seven stars which you saw in My right hand, and the seven golden lampstands, the seven stars are the angels of the seven churches, and the seven lampstands are the seven churches" (Revelation 1:17-20).

What are the proper responses to the awesome vision of Christ? We find them here in John's experience.

A REPENTANT HEART

First, a vision of the glorified Holy One brings an instant awareness of our own sinfulness. Only in seeing Christ for who He is do we see ourselves for who we are. Therefore, we are not surprised that John's first response was repentance and humble submission.

And when I saw Him, I fell at His feet (Revelation 1:17a).

Immediately, John collapsed to the ground, left to grovel on the floor. Every nerve fiber in his body was trembling. He was looking for a place to hide. *Anywhere* to get out from under the holy gaze of Christ.

But there was no place to hide. John lay naked before Christ. Undone. Unmasked. Unraveled.

The apostle realized that he was in the presence of the Holy One. He was before One infinitely greater than he. This awesome vision drove John to his knees. Terrified, he collapsed at Jesus' feet. His soul was overpowered. His spirit was overwhelmed. His heart was ripped to pieces. He buried his face in the dirt before Christ.

Why was John so humbled?

The aged apostle was looking upon unveiled Deity. No mortal man inhabiting sinful flesh can look upon God and live. He would burn up like a cinder!

God told Moses, "You cannot see My face, for no man can see Me and live!" (Exodus 33:20). No man can see God and live. No one. It would be easier to walk onto the surface of the sun than to walk into the presence of God's unveiled glory.

"We shall surely die, for we have seen God" (Judges 13:22), said Manoah. He knew he deserved to die because he had seen God.

Ezekiel's divine encounter was no different. The prophet saw heaven's throne, high and exalted, and upon it, he saw the figure of a man—the glorified, majestic Jesus Christ! His divine legs and feet were like burnished bronze glowing in a furnace. When Ezekiel saw Him, he dramatically collapsed to the ground like a building being demolished with dynamite (Ezekiel 1:22-28). Who could stand erect in the presence of a holy God?

Again Ezekiel saw Christ's glory. And again Ezekiel fell on his face (Ezekiel 3:22-23). He was brought low in instant submission. Humble prostration resulted.

Once more the prophet saw Christ's face shining like the sun. He heard Christ's voice like the sound of many waters. Overwhelmed, he collapsed to the ground before Christ (Ezekiel 43:2-3).

One final time, God revealed the glory of Christ to Ezekiel. And once more Ezekiel fell on his face (Ezekiel 44:4). Whenever he saw Christ's unveiled Deity—resplendent, bright, brilliant, blazing, blinding—he could only fall down before Him.

Saul of Tarsus did the same. As he traveled to Damascus, a light from heaven flashed around him. It was the blinding vision of Christ's glory. Instantly, Saul was knocked off his high horse. While lying in the dirt, he said, "Who art Thou, Lord?" Christ replied, "I am Jesus whom you are persecuting" (Acts 9:3-5). Instant submission. Humble prostration.

This was the Apostle John's experience. Upon seeing Christ's glory, the aged apostle did the same as others before him. He fell on his face before Christ.

A vision of the glorified Christ will always drive us to our knees. Humble submission will always result. Like John, we must find ourselves at His feet. Lower and lower we must descend, driven downward by His divine presence. Revival begins when we see Christ and instantly come to the end of ourselves. Only in utter submission before Christ can God begin to work in and through us.

Back to John. He collapsed to the ground upon seeing unveiled Deity. In that split second, he saw his own depravity. For the first time John saw himself for who he was. The holiness of Christ exposed John's own unholiness.

John caught one glimpse of the Holy One and his self-esteem was shattered. For the first time, he really understood who Christ was. In that moment, he also really understood his sinful heart.

It's always that way. When we see Christ as holy, we immediately see ourselves as unholy. Between His holiness and our unholiness is an infinite gulf. Until we understand His holiness, we will never know the depth of our own sin. When we compare ourselves with others, we seem *respectable*. But when we see ourselves in comparison to Him, we are *ruined*. Shaken down to our roots! The closer we draw to the Light, the more the dirt of our own heart is exposed.

Certainly, the conviction of sin produced Isaiah's response to the holy presence of God. "In the year of King Uzziah's death, I saw the Lord sitting on a throne, lofty and exalted, with the train of His robe filling the temple. Seraphim stood above Him, each having six wings; with two he covered his face, and with two he covered his feet, and with two he flew. And one called out to another and said, 'Holy, Holy, Holy, is the Lord of hosts, the whole earth is full of His glory.' And the foundations of the thresholds trembled at the voice of him who called out, while the temple was filling with smoke. Then I said, 'Woe is me, for I am *ruined*!'" (Isaiah 6:1-5).

He was saying, "I am a wretched sinner! Cursed and doomed am I!"

This was also Peter's experience. After a long day's fishing endeavor, Jesus told Simon to shove back out and let down his nets again. Simon snapped back, "Lord, You stick to the preaching and let us do the fishing."

Begrudgingly, Peter launched back out. But, to his amazement, his catch was so big that their nets began to break. Simon signaled to his partners in the other boat for help. They came, and soon both of their boats were filled with fish. So much so that both boats began to sink.

When Peter saw this, he realized he was standing in the presence of a holy God! His pride was painfully exposed, and his wretched heart was cut to the core. Instantly, he fell at Jesus' feet, confessing, "Depart from me, for I am a sinful man, O Lord!" (Luke 5:9).

He unraveled like a cheap sweater. No wonder that Peter later admonished us, "Clothe yourselves with humility toward one another, for God is opposed to the proud, but gives grace to the humble. Humble yourselves, therefore, under the mighty hand of God ..." (1 Peter 5:5-6). A once proud Peter learned humility at the feet of Jesus.

This was John's experience as well. When he saw this display of Christ's holiness, he saw what a wretched sinner he was. John collapsed to the ground, falling on his face before Christ. Instant submission. Humble prostration.

This is the posture of all those who see Christ's glory. Even today, believers who see the glorified Christ in the pages of Scripture are driven to their knees.

Corrie ten Boom was once asked if it was difficult for her to remain humble. Her reply was simple. "When Jesus rode into Jerusalem on Palm Sunday on the back of a donkey, and everyone was waving palm branches and throwing garments on the road and singing praises, do you think that for one moment it ever entered the head of that donkey that any of that was for him?"

Then she added, "If I can be the donkey on which Jesus Christ rides in His glory, I will give him all the praise and all the honor."

That's what we are. Lowly creatures on which the glory of God rides. We must never forget it.

What about *you*? Have you seen the depravity of your own heart? Have you been humbled low before the holiness of Christ? Have you ever fallen on your face before the Holy One?

This must be the posture of the church—flat on our faces before Christ. The church only advances on her knees.

A REVERENTIAL AWE

Second, a vision of the glorified Christ will instill a healthy, holy fear of God. Not only did John fall to the ground, but he did so in most dramatic fashion. He collapsed at Jesus' feet as *a dead man!*

The apostle was so overcome with fear that he fainted! He fell lifeless to the ground. He was absolutely speechless. Terrified. Trembling. Traumatized. Motionless. Stunned. Shocked. Shook up.

Years earlier, John had comfortably laid his head on Christ's bosom (John 13:25). But now, he disintegrates as a sinner in the presence of a holy God.

A little boy was to appear in his school's play. His one line was, "It is I; be not afraid." But he became so full of stage fright that when he came out on stage, all he blurted out was, "It's me and I'm scared to death!"

That's how John felt. He was speechless, spitless, and all shook up.

The fear of God always accompanies any true vision of Christ's glory. When the disciples beheld Christ's glory on the Mount of Transfiguration, they shook with fear. When He was transfigured before them, His face shone like the sun, and His garments became as white as light. How did they respond? "They fell on their faces and were much afraid" (Matthew 17:6).

Is fearing God a legitimate spiritual response?

Absolutely. At the very core of any true faith, there must be a healthy, holy fear of God that causes us to tremble. Please understand, this is not the dread a young boy feels when he sees the neighborhood bully walking toward him. Rather, it is the respect that a young boy would feel were he to stand before the President of the United States of America in the Oval Office. A fearful reverence and awe.

Godly fear is a sense of intimidation as we behold the holiness and power of Christ. It is a sense of awe as we perceive His majesty.

Jesus' presence always instilled a fear in people. People often trembled when they rightly understood His Deity. After Jesus calmed the violent storm, the disciples were terrified because they realized that a holy God was in their boat (Mark 4:41). The woman who touched the hem of His garment shook with terror when she grasped His glory (Mark 5:33).

Fearing God is the beginning of a true knowledge of God. "The fear of the Lord is the beginning of knowledge" (Proverbs 1:7). In fact, fearing God is the very essence of knowing Him.

The wisest man who ever lived, Solomon, wrote, "The fear of the Lord is the beginning of wisdom, and the knowledge of the Holy One is understanding" (Proverbs 9:10). This is a Hebrew parallelism. The fear of the Lord *is* the knowledge of the Holy One. To know Him *is* to fear Him.

Likewise, the bottom line of the Christian life is to fear God. Again, Solomon writes, "The conclusion, when all has been heard, is: fear God and keep His commandments, because this applies to every person" (Ecclesiastes 12:13). When we reduce life down to its lowest common denominator, the essence of a meaningful life is to fear God.

Bottom line? Fear God!

Consider Job. He was the most godly man of his day. At least that was God's estimation. The Lord said, "Have you considered My servant Job? For there is no one like Him on the earth, a blameless and upright man, fearing God and turning away from evil" (Job 1:8). Fearing God was the benchmark of spiritual maturity.

We have not rightly understood this vision of Christ until it has inspired fear in *our* hearts. His awesome presence must drive us to our knees. Again. And again. Better to be dead at Jesus' feet than alive anywhere else.

Charles Lamb once told Robert Browning, "If Shakespeare was to come into this room, we should all rise up to meet him, but if [Christ] was to come into it, we should all fall down and try to kiss the hem of His garment." That's the difference between common respect and reverential awe.

Let's face it. There's too little fear of God in our churches today. Everything is designed to take away such fear, not to shake us up. But a true vision of Christ will do just that. It will shake us down to the very core of our being.

A REASSURING PEACE

The Sovereign Lord now reaches out and places His hand upon the apostle. Is it over for John? Is this the end of John's life? Hardly.

This holy Christ is also a Christ of grace. Jesus refused to allow John to grovel long on his belly without comforting him. While shaking at His feet, something remarkable happens to John.

> And He laid His right hand upon me, saying, "Do not be afraid; I am the first and the last, and the living One; and I was dead, and behold, I am alive forevermore, and I have the keys of death and of Hades" (Revelation 1:17b-18).

As John lies limp at Jesus' feet, the omnipotent hand reaches out to restore his disintegrated soul. It is a touch of tender grace that brings reassuring comfort and peace. At this point, John needed to be reminded of Christ's healing mercy and strengthening grace.

Jesus often reached out and touched those in need. If it was a blind man, He would touch and heal his eyes. If it was a deaf man, He would reach out and touch his ears. If it was someone sick, Jesus would lay His hands upon the person and cure his or her illness. If it was a little baby, He would take the infant into His arms and bless the child. If it was a leper, He would touch the unclean man and instantly heal him. The touch of His hand brought His strengthening grace.

No wonder Jesus reaches out and touches John. The elderly apostle, now in his nineties, has almost died of a heart attack because the Lord unveiled His glory. He needs to be restored and reassured. In John's weakness, Christ's strength is now perfected (2 Corinthians 12:9-10).

What a contrast! The clenched fist that securely clutches the two-edged sword is now gently extended to comfort John. The holy heart beneath the golden sash is now moved with deep compassion. The blazing eyes of fire now look down favorably upon John. The stern voice of many waters now speaks gracious words of reassurance.

In order to comfort John, Christ gives a fuller revelation of Himself. True strength always comes from a deeper knowledge of Christ. What Jesus reveals about Himself here is so strengthening.

> *"I am the first and the last, and the living One; and I was dead, and behold, I am alive forevermore, and I have the keys of death and of Hades" (Revelation 1:17-18).*

Here are staggering claims for Deity, uttered by our Lord. The effect is, "John, look to Me and be comforted."

I AM

Surely, John must have remembered those two familiar words, "I am." It was John himself who recorded the series of "I am" claims in his Gospel narrative.

Years earlier John had recorded Jesus' words, "*I am* the bread of life" (John 6:35). "*I am* the light of the world" (John 8:12). "*I am* the door of the sheep" (John 10:7). "*I am* the good Shepherd" (John 10:11). "*I am* the resurrection, and the life" (John 11:35). "*I am* the way, and the truth, and the life" (John 14:6). "*I am* the true vine" (John 15:1).

"*I am*" was the divine name that God chose for Himself. It signifies His eternality, self-sufficiency, and gracious redemption. God told Moses to approach Pharaoh and say, "Let My people go." But Moses complained, "There are so many gods in Egypt. How will they know that the true and living God has sent me?"

God took a name for Himself that is above every other so-called god. He said, "Tell them that *I am that I am* sent you" (Exodus 3:14, paraphrased). This means, "I am the self-existent, eternal, sovereign God." Not "I was that I was." Nor, "I will be that I will be." But, "*I am that I am.*"

Now Jesus takes this divine name to identify Himself. In so doing, Jesus is claiming, in no uncertain terms, to be God!

Nothing brings strength to our souls like the name of God. Nothing.

THE FIRST AND THE LAST

Jesus claimed to be "the first and the last." This is another staggering claim for Deity!

Under the Old Covenant, God said, "I, the Lord, am the first, and with the last" (Isaiah 41:4). Again, "Thus says the Lord, the King of Israel, and His Redeemer, the Lord of hosts: 'I am the first and I am the last, and there is no God besides Me" (Isaiah 44:6). Also, "I am He, I am the first, I am also the last" (Isaiah 48:12). Now, under the New Covenant, here is Jesus saying, "I am the first and the last." Unequivocally, He is claiming to be truly God.

By saying, "I am the first," Christ lays claim to eternal preexistence. He claims to have existed from all eternity past. He is the uncreated One who predates all creation. John himself wrote, "In the beginning was the Word, and the Word was with God, and the Word was God. He was in the beginning with God. All things came into being through Him; and apart from Him nothing came into being that has come into being" (John 1:1-3).

Because Jesus is "the first," He is always previous. Everything is working according to His eternal decree (Ephesians 1:11).

As "the last," Christ is described as eternally immutable. He will rule without end throughout all eternity future. From everlasting to everlasting, He is God. He is the same "yesterday and today, yes and forever" (Hebrews 13:8). As "the last," Christ will have the final word. If His final call is refused, He will execute the *final* judgment.

THE LIVING ONE

Jesus says, "I am the living One" and assumes another divine name for Himself. This means that He is the source of all life. It is His prerogative to give or withhold all life.

This was a name applied to God. To Joshua, God said, "By this you shall know that *the living God* is among you" (Joshua 3:10). Peter used this name to describe God: "Thou art the Christ, the Son of *the living God*" (Matthew 16:16). Caiaphas said, "I adjure you by *the living God*, that you tell us whether You are the Christ" (Matthew 26:63).

But now Jesus Himself claims to *be* this living God when He says, "I am the living One." Clearly, He is saying, "I am God."

Moreover, Jesus claimed, "I was dead, and behold, I am alive forevermore." The living God dead? How can this be? The living God became a man and died on the cross for our sins. God did not cease to live, but Jesus the man died. Peter explained that Jesus was "put to death in the flesh, but made alive in the Spirit" (1 Peter 3:18).

Jesus is saying, "John, there's nothing to fear. I have conquered sin, death, Satan, and hell. I am alive forever."

THE KEEPER OF THE KEYS

Finally, Jesus says, "I have the keys of death and of Hades." "Death" signifies the condition of the dead, "Hades" the place. Christ's keys signify His sovereign authority to open and close the grave. He governs all access through the ironclad door of death. No one enters or leaves except by His divine authority. Jesus possesses authority over death to admit people into the grave. He decides *who* dies *when*. And He alone can get them out.

This is tantamount to saying, "I have all power over death. I am the resurrection and the life. No one dies except by divine appointment."

This is a great encouragement to John. Although about ninety years old, Christ is not yet finished with him. His life is not yet over. As he lies like a dead man on the ground, John may feel like he is about to die. But Jesus is not yet ready to open the door of death to admit him. The time for his departure has not yet come.

So, what did Jesus still have for John to do?

A RESTORED MINISTRY

Fourth, a vision of Christ's glory will always renew us in our ministry. Seeing the glory of Christ brings a great responsibility. Having seen Christ's majesty, John is now commissioned to communicate

HOLY TERROR

that glory to others. Necessity is laid upon him. Witnessing this awesome vision mandates telling others. So, John is now admonished by Christ, a second time, to write it down.

> *"Write therefore the things which you have seen, and the things which are and the things which shall take place after these things" (Revelation 1:19).*

Actually, John is told to record three things. First, the apostle is to write down "the things which you have seen"—the awesome vision of Christ (Revelation 1). Second, he is to record "the things which are"—the seven letters to the seven churches (Revelation 2—3). Third, he must write down "the things which shall take place after these things"—the prophetic future surrounding Christ's return (Revelation 4—22). That's the divine outline for Revelation.

What a ministry assignment! John is commissioned by Christ to write in a book—the book of Revelation—the awesome vision of Christ. He is told to record the final call of Christ to the church. Just when John thinks his days of ministry are over, Christ calls him to embark on his most significant ministry task yet.

Jesus says, "Get up, John. Do what I've called you to do! Don't keep this vision to yourself. Write it down in a book."

R. C. Sproul writes, "There is a pattern, a pattern repeated over and over in history. God appears, man quakes in terror, God forgives and heals, God sends. From brokenness to mission is the pattern for man."

Christ restores John, putting him back together, and uses this shattered man to record His final call to the churches. Before God uses any man greatly, He first breaks him deeply. Only then is His glory safe with a man. John is now a broken man ready to be used by Christ.

Here is the Great Commission of the book of Revelation. Under divine mandate, John is told to communicate this awesome vision of Christ to all nations.

This is our responsibility as well. We, too, must tell others about our glorious Lord. As Billy Graham says, "Don't keep the faith—*share* it!"

I heard about a man who envisioned the following scene. When

Jesus ascended to heaven, the angels asked him, "Did You accomplish Your task?"

"Yes, all is finished," the Lord replied.

"We have a second question," said the angels. "Has the whole world heard of You?"

"No," said Jesus.

The angels then asked, "Then, what is Your plan?"

Jesus said, "I have left twelve men and some other followers to carry the message to the whole world."

The angels looked at Him and asked, "What is your Plan B?"

There is no Plan B! Plan A is still in force. We are to tell the whole world about Christ and call them to faith in Him. Jesus has decided to reach the world through His church. We who have seen the glorified Christ must tell the world!

A RENEWED MIND

Finally, this vision of Christ imparted deeper spiritual understanding to John. By no coincidence, Christ now reveals the first of many mysteries in this book to John. It is while he is laying flat on his face that the apostle gains a better understanding of truth. So, Christ says:

> *"As for the mystery of the seven stars which you saw in My right hand, and the seven golden lampstands, the seven stars are the angels of the seven churches, and the seven lampstands are the seven churches"* (Revelation 1:20).

The brilliant light of Christ's glory enabled John to see God's Word more clearly. A "mystery" is now revealed to John.

What is a *mystery*? It is something secret or hidden that is beyond the reach of natural human understanding. A mystery can only be grasped through special revelation from God's Spirit. If a mystery is truth concealed, then revelation is truth revealed.

Christ now explains, "the seven stars are the angels of the seven churches." These "stars," or "angels," are the spiritual leaders of these local churches—the pastors or elders. Like stars, pastors are to shine forth the light of God's Word. Like angels, they are messengers sent by God to communicate His truth.

Jesus further identifies, "the seven lampstands are the seven churches." Again, the focus is that, like lampstands, the churches are to bear God's light in a dark world. The church is to be a lighthouse along a jagged, rocky coastline, guiding tempest-tossed lives into the safe harbor of God's grace.

John saw more truth on his face than he could on his feet. Only humble, God-fearing people are able to more clearly see spiritual truth. God has hidden His truth from the wise and the prudent and has revealed it unto babies (Matthew 11:25). The proud of heart walk with their noses too high in the air to see truth.

Spiritual understanding comes to the humble. Only those who are flat on their faces before Christ can grasp divine mysteries. God does not reveal His deeper truths to proud, carnal, self-reliant people (1 Corinthians 3:1-3). That would be like putting a lighted stick of dynamite into the hand of a chimpanzee. They would know enough to be dangerous. Their heads would exceed their hearts.

Deeper insight into truth is reserved for God-fearing believers in whose hands God's glory is safe. If you are having trouble understanding God's truth, get on your knees.

These are the marks of the one who has been in the presence of Jesus Christ. A repentant heart. A reverential awe. A reassuring peace. A restored ministry. A renewed mind. This was John's experience. And so must it be ours.

Has a holy terror gripped your heart? Have you been overwhelmed by the glory of Jesus Christ? Is your heart filled with reverence for Christ?

This *must* be the position of the church. Flat on its face before her Lord. Broken. Humbled. Convicted. Contrite. Fearful. Awestruck. Touched. Reassured. Comforted. Strengthened. Commissioned. Focused. Empowered. Renewed. Illumined. Revitalized.

Before we can hear, apply, and obey the final call revealed in the seven letters to the seven churches, we must first be brought low at the feet of Christ.

Not too long ago, Queen Elizabeth paid a visit to the United States. She was accompanied by her royal entourage, advance team, and Her Majesty's Secret Service.

While visiting in Los Angeles, Her Highness was driven through some of the most underprivileged neighborhoods. As she approached one project area in a lesser ghetto, she unexpectedly asked her limousine driver to stop. When he did, she got out of the automobile unannounced and went into a very poor apartment chosen at random.

The lady of the house was overwhelmed. The Queen of England in her humble abode! Unaware of the proper protocol appropriate for addressing royalty, she did not know to curtsy or bow. Nor did she know to address the Queen as Her Majesty.

Instead, when she naively approached England's Monarch, she wrapped both arms around her, giving the Queen a warm bear hug.

The Queen's entourage was appalled. The media was shocked. The Secret Service was aghast. No one touches the Queen.

This common woman was clueless. She had no idea how to address royalty. There was no fear. No awe. No reverence. Consequently, her approach was entirely inappropriate.

Too often that is the case in the church today. We have forgotten how to approach our King. No fear. No awe. No reverence.

May we be careful not to come into His presence with a careless, frivolous attitude. Instead, we must approach Him with reverence, awe, and humble adoration. Let us fall at His feet as dead men and prostrate ourselves before Him.

May *holy terror* fill the church again!

THE LETTERS OF JESUS CHRIST

REVELATION 2–3

INTRODUCTION
TO THE SEVEN LETTERS

CHURCHES ARE LIKE PEOPLE. No two are alike. Each has its own individual personality. Each comes in a different size and shape. Each has its own different strengths and weaknesses. Each lives in a different place.

That was true in the first century. As Jesus addressed the seven churches of Revelation 2–3, no two were alike. Each church had its own identity. Its own personality.

Consequently, what Jesus has to say to each church is unique. Each letter is tailored to fit the specific needs, strengths, and weaknesses of each congregation.

Each letter follows a common pattern:

   I. THE SETTING: Jesus will first identify each church by the city in which it ministers.

  II. THE SPEAKER: Each letter then has a unique description of Jesus Christ, the Author of these letters, that is fitted appropriately to the needs of that church.

 III. THE STRENGTHS: The Lord commends each church—except for Laodicea—for particular areas of faithfulness in serving Him.

 IV. THE SIN: Each church is admonished, sometimes severely, for areas of compromise and carnality. There are two exceptions—Smyrna and Philadelphia, the two most persecuted churches.

  V. THE SOLUTION: In the shadow of each rebuke, Jesus prescribes the solution that will restore that church to spiritual health. In each case, it is the same prescription—a call to repentance.

 VI. THE SUFFERING: Two churches, Smyrna and Philadelphia, are unusually suffering persecution because of their public confession. Jesus' encouragement will greatly strengthen these people.

VII. THE SUMMONS: Jesus calls every believer in every church in every place to hear what the Spirit has said in that letter and to put it into practice.

VIII. THE SUCCESS: In order to motivate us to faithfulness, the Lord holds before each church a promise of future blessing in heaven.

What is the value of these seven letters?

First, these letters help us examine our own churches. The same strengths and weaknesses as in these first-century churches can be found in your church today. If so, then Christ's solution is what your church needs.

In a day that has seen the proliferation of church consultants and how-to seminars, we need to recognize the preeminent Church Consultant, Jesus Christ—the rightful Head of the church. He alone has promised to build His church.

Second, these seven letters have application to our own lives. Christ will speak to you personally through each of these letters. The strengths and sins attributed to these churches may be found in your life. If so, you need to hear His counsel and follow it.

Ultimately, the final call to the churches in Asia Minor was a call to revival. It was a call to spiritual awakening. The Lord desired to restore the purity, the doctrine, and the spiritual fervor of His people. His desire has not changed. He wants *revival* in His churches. He wants *revival* in you and me!

"He who has an ear,
let him hear what the Spirit says
to the churches."

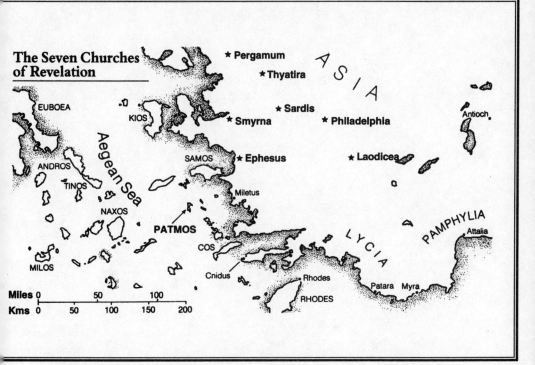

The Seven Churches of Revelation

★ Pergamum
★ Thyatira
★ Sardis
★ Philadelphia
★ Smyrna
★ Ephesus
★ Laodicea

EUBOEA
KIOS
ANDROS
TINOS
Aegean Sea
NAXOS
SAMOS
Miletus
PATMOS
COS
MILOS
Cnidus
RHODES
Rhodes

ASIA
Antioch
LYCIA
PAMPHYLIA
Attalia
Patara Myra

Miles 0   50   100
Kms 0   50   100   150   200

Taken from the NIV Study Bible. Copyright © 1985 by the Zondervan Corporation. Used by permission.

IV

YOU'VE LOST THAT LOVIN' FEELIN'

Revelation 2:1–7

EVERY EYE ON THE PLANET was riveted upon this real-life Cinderella story. It was the wedding of the century. They were the very definition of romance. The epitome of love, courtship, and marriage.

With 750 million viewers watching around the globe via satellite, the world's most eligible bachelor—Prince Charles, Duke of Windsor—exchanged wedding vows with a British aristocrat—the beautiful Lady Diana Spencer. All the world swooned as these two lived out the fantasy of multiplied millions.

It was all something out of a fairy tale. A starry-eyed script that could have been written in Hollywood. There was all the pomp and circumstance you would expect of a royal wedding—and more.

The date was July 29, 1981. The scene was St. Paul's Cathedral in London. With England's social elite present and Her Majesty's highest ranking dignitaries in attendance, Prince Charles stood at the front of the church, dressed in full military splendor, awaiting his bride. Down the long center aisle proceeded Lady Diana, dressed in an exquisite, long-flowing wedding dress. As the royal couple exchanged vows, they pledged their unconditional commitment and unwavering loyalty to each other.

When the high-churched ceremony was over, the newlyweds descended down the front steps of St. Paul's Cathedral. With every church bell in London chiming, they mounted the horse-drawn, gold-encrusted royal coach to ride off into the sunset.

The streets of London were lined with thousands of admirers, all craning their necks to get just a glimpse of the newly wedded royal couple. As the two dashed off to their honeymoon, they were so much in love. So full of life. So full of hope.

But that was *then*.

And something tragic happened.

The clock struck twelve on this real-life Cinderella story. Somewhere along the way their lives grew apart. Their love grew strangely cold. Stale. Stagnant. Mechanical. And routine. The storybook relationship had become sadly commonplace and ordinary.

Façades were erected. Pleasantries were exchanged. Public appearances were made. But it was all for show. Their passion was now ancient history. A thing of the past.

Tabloid reports were confirmed when on December 9, 1992, British Prime Minister John Major cleared his throat and broke the disheartened news to the House of Commons. Tragically, there would be a royal separation. Not a divorce, mind you. Just a mutual coexistence. A truce.

The Royal Highnesses would remain legally married and keep their royal positions. But they would now live in separate houses, lead separate lives, and go their separate ways. Occasionally they would attend national events together, but only for show.

The fact is, the honeymoon is over. The glow is gone. The royal romance is a thing of the past. England's most celebrated romance has become a national disgrace.

Far greater than the much-publicized romance between Prince Charles and Lady Di is our relationship with Jesus Christ. Ours is the greatest love story ever known. The King of kings courted us, lowly peasants that we were, and pursued us to become His royal bride. At first, we were the very definition of romance. The epitome of love, courtship, and marriage.

Our hearts were so full of passion and excitement. Bible study was so life-changing. Prayer was so heart-lifting. Worship was so earthshaking. We savored every moment in His presence.

But that was *then*.

And something tragic has happened.

Our love for Jesus Christ—passionate, vibrant, dynamic—is at the very core of what it means to be a Christian. To know Christ *is* to love Him. We love Him because He first loved us. Our personal relationship with Him is marked by intimacy, closeness, and mutual sharing.

But, as in any relationship, our love for Christ is subject to fluctuation. And sometimes there is a serious waning of our intensity. Sometimes our passion for the Lord grows stale. Stagnant. Mechanical. Routine. And we begin to take Him for granted.

The red-hot embers of our love for Christ can lose their radiant glow. Sure, we are still the bride of Jesus Christ. And, legally, we are still married. But we are merely coexisting. We share the same heart, but the relationship has grown cold. Hollow. Empty. Distant.

How about *you*? Is *your* love for Christ still strong? Is your enthusiasm still there? Or have you cooled off? Has the glow gone?

Sadly, such a separation happened to some believers in the first century. The believers at Ephesus had left their first love. Not in total, but in part. Once on fire for Christ, their blazing passion had cooled off to a flickering flame. Once extremely intimate, they were now distant from Him. So, Jesus—out of love for this church—seeks to restore their spiritual fervor. Our Lord takes the initiative to call them back to restore their relationship. He always takes the first step back toward us.

Here we will see how to recharge our spiritual batteries when they have gone flat.

THE SETTING

A trip to ancient Ephesus was like traveling today to New York City or Los Angeles. It was a busy, thriving metropolis by the end of the first century A.D.—the most prominent city in Asia Minor.

Located on the Caster River just three miles from the Aegean Sea, Ephesus was the major commerce center of Asia. Merchandise would be shipped across the Mediterranean Sea and up the Caster River to Ephesus, where the goods would be distributed to the known world.

Ephesus stood at the crossroads of travel. Four major highways intersected at Ephesus, bringing businessmen and merchants from the important cities of the Roman provinces. Likewise, the people there were very culturally advanced. They had all the amenities of a cosmopolitan city—sports, the arts, drama, and pageantry. This was no hick town!

Ephesus was called a "free city." Because of their loyalty to the Empire, the city was allowed to be self-governing. There was no Roman garrison present. No oppressive Roman shadow loomed over this town. As a result, it was a free-thinking place independent of overt Roman influence and tyranny.

Ephesus was also a center of pagan worship. One of the seven wonders of the ancient world was located here in Ephesus—the Temple of Diana. A place of heathen worship and idolatry, the Temple of Diana was a massive structure as long as two football fields. On the inside, pagan worship flourished with all its temple prostitution, the grossest perversions, drunkenness, and sexual orgies. Small wonder businessmen traveled the four major highways to Ephesus. They came flocking into the Temple of Diana to have their every sexual fantasy fulfilled.

Inside the Temple, criminals found political asylum from the long arm of Roman law. It became a haven for every known criminal, felon, and pervert. With prostitutes, eunuchs, dancers, and singers leading the "worshipers," Ephesus was a virtual cesspool of iniquity.

It was there, in the midst of that godless city, that God planted a thriving church. It is better to run a mission at the gates of hell than to preach to the choir. God often builds His church where the circumstances seem the least favorable. That's the grace of God.

THE SPEAKER

It is to this church in such an idolatrous and immoral setting that Jesus writes this letter. It is to this congregation that Jesus chooses to identify Himself in the following way:

> *"To the angel of the church in Ephesus write: 'The One who holds the seven stars in His right hand, the One who walks among the seven golden lampstands, says this: . . .'"* (Revelation 2:1).

Although this Speaker is not specifically named, it is obviously Jesus Christ. He is the same One revealed to John in the startling vision of Patmos. It is the Lord Himself dictating and dispatching this letter.

Jesus communicates this letter to "the angel of the church." The word *angel* means messenger and refers to the one whose primary ministry is to carry this message to the Ephesian congregation. Today we would call him the pastor or teaching elder. It is through the pastor that this message is to be brought to the church.

How does Jesus reveal Himself to this flock?

HOLDING SEVEN STARS

First, Jesus is the One holding the seven stars. Held firmly in His right hand, Jesus exercises direct control over seven shining celestial bodies. John has already interpreted for us the identity of the seven stars. They are the seven angels of the seven churches (Revelation 1:20). Each church has an angel, or messenger, who functions as the primary spiritual leader over that congregation. These men are called to lead the churches by communicating God's Word to His people. As the primary spiritual leaders of those flocks, they are entrusted with the ministry of the biblical teaching, pastoral care, and spiritual guidance.

Our Lord holds these men in His right hand—the place of strictest accountability, strongest protection, and most strategic usefulness. The word *hold* indicates keeping all of something in one's hand, like grasping a small stone or coin within one's fist. In His right hand, these spiritual leaders are surrounded and encompassed by Christ's care. As such, they are directly answerable to and completely controlled by Him. He alone has chosen them, and He uses them as it pleases Him.

Every spiritual leader—whether a pastor, elder, missionary, Bible study leader, or father—is similarly accountable to God. All who communicate His Word are directly accountable to Christ.

INSPECTING THE CHURCH

Second, Jesus walks among the lampstands. As the Lord of the church, He is the One walking among the lampstands. This on-location inspection keeps Him intimately involved in the life of each church. He walks the aisles and surveys the pews of every church. He walks into its classrooms and sits in boardrooms. There are no secrets before Him. He is constantly taking stock of His churches—auditing, assessing, inspecting, weighing, evaluating, and observing their spiritual condition.

So, to this Ephesian church, Christ pictures Himself as the One possessing absolute authority and control over the church's leadership and keeping a watchful eye with vigilance over the congregation.

THE STRENGTHS

Ephesus was one extraordinary church! We are not surprised that Jesus begins this letter by commending the believers there. While walking around their lampstand, there were many strengths for which Christ praises them.

> *"I know your deeds and your toil and perseverance, and that you cannot endure evil men, and you put to the test those who call themselves apostles, and they are not, and you found them to be false; and you have perseverance and have endured for My name's sake, and have not grown weary"* (Revelation 2:2-3).

At the core of their greatness was their dynamic ministry. This was a hard-working group of believers, constantly serving Christ. Not a museum for passive saints, but an infantry for active duty.

Christianity was no spectator sport here. They didn't come to church to be entertained. They were actively involved in the work of ministry. Sacrificially. Selflessly. Serving. Doing. Toiling. Giving. Going.

TOIL AND PERSEVERANCE

Jesus said, "I know all about your toil and perseverance." "Toil" (*kopas*) means that they served Christ to the point of exhaustion. Holy sweat rolled down their foreheads as they ministered in His name. "Perseverance" (*hupomone*) means they ministered under much stress and pressure. When they took on a task, they stuck with it until the job was finished.

These people were self-starters. Motivated. Active. Teaching the

Bible. Reaching souls. Supporting one another. Feeding the poor. Doing the ministry right and left. No lazy, lethargic members here.

This quality is very Christlike. Jesus came not to be served, but to serve (Mark 10:45). He laid down His life for others. His earthly life was full of good deeds, selfless toil, long days, draining hours, exerting Himself to the point of exhaustion. He served tirelessly during the days of His ministry.

STRICT AND SOUND

Second, this church would not "endure evil men." They set a high moral standard and chose not to tolerate sin in the camp. With holy zeal, they purged out evil with a vengeance. Morality was black and white here, with very little gray.

If one of their members slipped into sin, they would approach that person, lovingly confront him, and call him to repentance. If that person wouldn't repent, the church wouldn't allow this leaven to spread to the whole lump. Like operating on a deadly cancer, they eliminated sin wherever they found it.

Church here was no spiritual country club. They didn't look like saints on Sunday and act like aint's on Monday. They were serious about their walk with Christ.

Does your church "endure evil men"? Does it tolerate wickedness in the lives of its members? Has it committed itself to the exercise of church discipline?

Likewise, Jesus commended them, "You put to the test those who call themselves apostles, and they are not, and you found them to be false." When traveling teachers came to Ephesus, their doctrine was put to the test before they could get into the pulpit. The Ephesians had been well grounded in sound doctrine and were theologically discriminating. Doctrinal error would not be tolerated here.

They called a spade a spade. They could smell a heretic a mile off. When they heard theological error, alarms went off. Flares went up. False teachers were given an apple and a road map.

This shouldn't surprise us. The Ephesian church, by now forty years old, had enjoyed a long history of excellent Bible teaching. It was founded by the Apostle Paul (Acts 18:19-21), and the believers were discipled by Aquila (Acts 18:26), taught by Apollos (Acts 18:24-25), pastored by Timothy (1 Timothy 1:3), and instructed by the Apostle John. Either directly or indirectly, they had been the recipients of eight New Testament books: John, Ephesians, 1 and 2 Timothy, 1, 2, and 3 John, and Revelation. Likewise, Paul was in Ephesus when he wrote 1 Corinthians.

This was a citadel of orthodoxy! A bastion of truth. A fortress for the faith.

Is that important? Absolutely. The church that stands for nothing will fall for anything. Any ministry can only be as strong as its doctrinal purity. Like the foundation of a house, theological correctness provides stability, strength, and longevity.

We live in a day in which churches are built upon theological jello. We have divorced ourselves from the queen of the sciences—theology—in our affair with the behavioral sciences—psychology and sociology. We have sacrificed doctrinal purity on the altar of theological tolerance. *God, forgive us!*

STEADFAST AND STRONG

Jesus said, "You have perseverance and have endured for My name's sake, and have not grown weary" (verse 3). Despite growing opposition to Christ, this church remained rock-solid. They wouldn't waver from their mission. While living in the hub of paganism, they held tenaciously to their witness for Christ. Even when they caught flak for their convictions, there was no backing down! Not here. Even their motives were right. They endured for Christ's name's sake, not their own. They served for His glory, not their own reputation.

This is one dynamic church!

We need more congregations like this. Toiling. Persevering. Strict. Sound. Steadfast. And strong. They had all the right stuff. If you attended one of their church services, you would immediately sense you were with God's spiritual Marines. The few, the proud, the Ephesians.

They had something for everyone. Ministries were abounding. People were plugged in. Programs were busting loose. The place was hopping! What could possibly be wrong with a church like this?

Plenty.

They had *everything* but the *main* thing.

THE SIN

Abruptly, Jesus changes the tone of this letter. The Master puts His finger on the one glaring deficiency in this church that threatened to ruin everything else. He must address a fatal flaw—a deadly sin—so serious that it endangered the church's very existence. What could it possibly be? Jesus said:

> *"But I have this against you, that you have left your first love"*
> *(Revelation 2:4).*

This rebuke—"But I have this against you"—sends a bone-chilling tingle up my spine every time I read it. It always hurts when someone has something against you. But when Jesus does, that's serious!

Something was missing. This church had left its first love. Amid the Ephesians' many ministries and their tenacious stand for the truth, their love for Christ had grown cold. The more busy they became, the further they drifted away from simple devotion to Christ.

First love is the fervent, passionate, red-hot love of a newly wedded couple. It pictures the romantic love that a couple feels when they first start dating. A chemistry happens. A mystical attraction occurs. Two hearts heat up. A romance inflames. Two lives fall in love, get married, and become one.

But something happens along the way. Somewhere in the daily routine of marriage, the honeymoon ceases. The children come. The career takes off. The business expands. The activities increase. The stresses multiply. And suddenly two people wake up complete strangers.

This slow leak is what left Ephesus flat. Their devoted love for Christ had cooled off. Their ministry had become mechanical. Their relationship had become routine. Doxology slipped back into cold orthodoxy. They were still coming to church. They were still serving. And they were still believing rightly. But their hearts were no longer in it. They had lots of activity *for* Christ, but little intimacy *with* Christ. They had full heads, busy feet, but empty hearts.

This cooling off always happens over time. "Left" pictures a gradual release. It means to leave something behind over a period of time. This departure didn't happen overnight. Somewhere along the way, they lost their passion.

I'm reminded of the couple who were driving home from church. The wife was sitting in the front seat on the far right side. Her husband was in his usual place behind the steering wheel. Seemingly, a large gulf separated them.

With lonely eyes, she looked at him and said, "Honey, do you remember when we first met, how close we used to sit to each other? You used to put your arm around me. What happened to those days?"

With one hand firmly attached to the steering wheel, and the other resting on the empty seat between them, he said, "Well, I haven't moved."

The distance was not because *he* had moved. A separation resulted because *she* had moved away. She had left her first love.

That's precisely what had happened in the Ephesian church. Over the years, they had left their first love. They had backslidden away from Christ.

Ladies, imagine that your husband came home and said, "I don't love you anymore. But nothing will change. I'll still earn a living and pay the bills. We'll still sit together and sleep together. I'll still father our children. I just don't love you anymore." Would that be good enough for you?

No way. You would be devastated. Yet, we say that to the Lord. "Jesus, I don't love You like I once did. But I'll still come to church. I'll still serve You. I'll still witness for You. I just don't love You."

That's not good enough for Jesus either! He wants a relationship, not a performance. Jesus says, "Your heart has grown cold toward Me. You have left your first love." Is this serious?

Absolutely. Jesus said that the greatest commandment is to love God (Matthew 22:37-39). We must love Him with all of our heart, soul, mind, and strength. Love for Christ must fill every inch of our being. Without love for Him, we are just "a noisy gong or a clanging cymbal" (1 Corinthians 13:1). Our hearts must pulsate with a blazing, passionate, vibrant love for Christ or we are nothing.

If we fail to love Him, we disobey the greatest commandment. It doesn't matter what else we obey, if we fail to keep the highest commandment. We have struck out! Leaving our first love is the greatest sin.

If our love for Christ is cold, it doesn't matter how faithfully we serve Him. Or how rightly we believe. Or how strongly we stand. If you miss first base, it doesn't matter how far you hit the ball, nor how many bases you touch. If you miss first base, you're out. O - U - T! If you leave your first love, you're out of His favor.

How about *you*? Is your spiritual honeymoon over? Is your passion gone? Has your love faded? If so, you have left your first love.

In the anonymity of the crowd, it's easy to play the church game. To attend the right Bible study. To use the right lingo. To run with the right group. You can fake it. Even cover it up. But the more you do, the emptier you feel. There's a gnawing feeling deep inside. You have drifted further away from the Lord. And you *know* it!

So, what are we to do?

How can we recapture our first love?

THE SOLUTION

With a yearning heart, Jesus now pleads with the Ephesian church. With arms wide open, He prescribes the steps that lead back to the honeymoon stage. Practically speaking, here is how we again draw close to Him! Here is how to rekindle our lost passion for Christ. Here's how to fall back in love with Christ. Jesus said:

> "Remember therefore from where you have fallen, and repent and do the deeds you did at first; or else I am coming to you, and will remove your lampstand out of its place—unless you repent. Yet this you do have, that you hate the deeds of the Nicolaitans, which I also hate" (Revelation 2:5-6).

STEP ONE: REMEMBER

First, Jesus says, "*Remember* from where you have fallen." In other words, remember back to when you first came to faith in Christ. Replay that initial excitement. Refocus on those times when you really loved Jesus.

Can you remember when you first fell in love with Christ? Can you recall when you were on fire? You were so excited and full of passion. Every time you opened the Word of God, it had something to say to you. Whenever you prayed, all heaven seemed to open up to you! Wherever you went, you had to tell people about Him. Wherever you saw a need, you ministered in the name of Christ. Christ had done so much for you, you *had* to serve Him!

Can you remember a time like that?

I can. When I was in high school, I went to a Young Life camp in Colorado. I can still hear the camp speaker talking about Jesus turning the water to wine. Just as Christ turned dirty, dingy, stagnant water into sparkling, red wine, Jesus could do the same with my life. He could transform my life into the very best life possible!

After hearing that message, I walked into the cool, brisk, Colorado mountain air and looked up at the starry skies overhead. I was overwhelmed with the majesty of God. How could a God so big love me? My heart wanted to burst, I was so excited for God! I told Christ that I wanted to know and love Him all my life.

Can you *remember* a time like that?

Later, when I was in college, I would sit up late in my dorm room, reading God's Word. Christ was so real! God was so alive! I carried my Bible to class and read it between classes. I underlined the verses that spoke directly to my heart. It seemed like my entire New Testament was underlined! I was so on fire for Christ!

Can you *remember* a time like that?

After I graduated from college, I attended a dynamic church in Memphis, Tennessee. Every time they opened the church's doors, I was sitting in the middle of the front row. Everything the preacher had to say was for me. I shed tears when the choir sang. The Holy Spirit tugged on my heart when people were saved.

Can you *remember* a time like that?

For some of us, such a time was only three months ago. For others, it was three years ago. For others, ten years ago.

The road back to Christ begins by, first, *remembering*. Memory is the handmaid of revival. Remember the joy that was yours with Him. Can't you recall those times when you first really loved Christ? Get a good look at when you were on fire for Him. Can you remember the pit from which you were dug?

That's where revival begins—*remember!*

STEP TWO: REPENT

Second, Jesus says, *"Repent."* After you remember, repent! Repentance means to change the direction of your life. It is a change of heart. A change of mind. A change of will. It means to head back to the way things once were. It is a turning around and coming back to Christ.

The fact is, something or someone has replaced your first love. It's not that you don't have a first love anymore. It's that you have a *new* first love. It's no longer Christ.

Anything that you love more than you love Christ is your new first love. It may be your job. It could be a relationship. Or your education. Or your house. Or your family. Whatever. It's anything or anyone that you are more excited about than you are about Christ.

Repent! Change your life. Pursue a new direction. Get on your knees and confess your spiritual apathy. Turn your cold heart back to Christ. As a decisive act of your will, choose to change your heart.

Say, "God, my heart has been distant from You. I've been far away from You. Lord, I want to change. Jesus, I'm turning my life around right now. Right now, I'm rededicating my life afresh to You. God, I want the passion for You back in my life."

James put it this way. "Draw near to God and He will draw near to you" (4:8). If we will take the first step back to God, He will meet us more than halfway.

STEP THREE: REPEAT

Third, Jesus says, "do the deeds you did at first." They were told to *repeat* the spiritual activities they did at the first. In other words, "Get back to the basics." What are these first deeds? Jesus doesn't specifically tell us here, but we can discover what they are from other New Testament Scriptures.

Simply put, these first deeds are what the early believers did when they were first saved and added to the church. After Peter preached on the day of Pentecost, 3,000 souls were converted, baptized, and enfolded into the church. Immediately, these new believers were "continually devoting themselves to the apostles' teaching and to fellowship, to the breaking of bread and to prayer" (Acts 2:42).

These are the first deeds to which these first Christians devoted themselves —teaching, fellowship, worship, and prayer.

They studied the *apostles' teaching*. Their daily staple was the basic doctrinal truths taught by the apostles. Biblical truth is essential to the health of every believer. It is the Word of God that stimulates our hearts to love Christ. The Word inflames passion for Christ. The early disciples remarked, "Were not our hearts burning within us while He was . . . explaining the Scriptures to us?" (Luke 24:32).

They maintained close *fellowship*. They were continually sharing and encouraging one another. Bearing one another's burdens. Comforting one another's hearts.

They came together to *break bread*. The early church worshiped Christ by regularly taking the Lord's Supper together. Communion with the living Christ kept their hearts aflame. The Lord's Table cultivated reverence, gratitude, purity, and the anticipation of Christ's return.

They devoted themselves to *prayer*. These early disciples spent much time on their knees. Kneeling in God's presence was as necessary as breathing. Daily, they enjoyed intimate fellowship with Him. After all, seven days without prayer makes one weak. Prayer personalizes our Bible study. It transforms God's truth into personal devotion to Christ. It keeps us fervent for our first love.

If you have left your first love, get back to the basics. Get back to Bible study. Get back into the fellowship. Get back to worship. Get back on your knees in prayer. These spiritual disciplines lead us back to full love for Christ. In Scripture, we hear from Christ. In fellowship, we share Christ. At the Lord's Table, we commune with Christ. In prayer, we talk to Christ. These spiritual basics always bring us back to Christ!

If they would not take these steps back to Christ, He adds, "I am coming to you, and will remove your lampstand out of its place—unless you repent." In other words, "If you lose your first love for Me, you will eventually lose your lampstand." That's serious! No love, no light.

This coming of Christ is not the Second Coming. It is a special coming of visitation, in judgment and discipline. If they will not return to their first love, Jesus will extinguish their light. This pictures a loss of their testimony and witness. Jesus threatens to blow out their light.

Tragically, this has already happened with many churches. The congregation still meets Sunday by Sunday. The Finance Committee still oversees the budget month by month. The people still serve day by day. But there is no light transmitted.

Jesus says, "Turn out the lights, the party's over."

STEP FOUR: REMAIN

Fourth, Jesus says, "Yet, this you do have, that you hate the deeds of the Nicolaitans which I also hate" (verse 6). Jesus concludes by telling them to *remain* in the battle against sin. They are to remain true to the faith and resist false teaching.

Note how sensitive Jesus' heart is toward this church. He guards against deflating them by concluding with a note of praise: "You hate the deeds of the Nicolaitans, which I also hate." In essence, Jesus is saying, "We're on the same team. We are a lot alike. We both hate the deeds of the Nicolaitans. Keep at it!"

What are "the deeds of the Nicolaitans"? In a nutshell, these men were itinerant teachers who taught antinomian (no law) sin—a dangerous heresy that encouraged moral license. They taught that a Christian can live however he or she pleases. Grace covers everything. There are no consequences to sin. (We will examine the teaching of the Nicolaitans more in depth in a later chapter.)

Do you see the four critical steps? Each leads back to Christ. *Remember . . . repent . . . repeat . . . remain!* Each step rekindles our first love for Christ.

THE SUMMONS

Jesus concludes with a command to all believers. Every word of Scripture calls for our obedience. But here, Jesus makes a special appeal for every believer to heed His Word.

> *"He who has an ear, let him hear what the Spirit says to the churches"*
> *(Revelation 2:7a).*

Webster defines *summons* as "to call upon for specified action." Here, Jesus issues a summons to all the "churches"—note the plural. This call is for *every* church in *every* age. It's for *every* believer—note the singular ("he, and him"). This invitation is for *all* believers in *all* churches in *all* times.

The summons here is to pay special attention to what Jesus has just said by the Holy Spirit. He invites us to carefully hear and decisively heed the message. These truths are critically important!

Have you left your first love?

Many churches today are like the Ephesian church. They are marked by doctrinal zeal. Faithful service. Pure living. A bold stand for truth. But such fervency is often accompanied by a loss of one's first love. All too often, an increase in programs and activities breeds a decrease in love for Christ.

Have you left your first love? Has your heart grown cold? Have you become too busy to spend time with Him? If so, take deliberate steps to be alone with Him. Make definite plans to recapture your first love.

THE SUCCESS

To those believers who will overcome their spiritual apathy and return to their first love, Jesus makes a great promise.

> *"To him who overcomes, I will grant to eat of the tree of life, which is in the Paradise of God" (Revelation 2:7b)*

Specifically, this promise is addressed to the *overcomer*. Every true believer in Jesus Christ is an overcomer. Scripture says, "And who is the one who overcomes the world, but he who believes that Jesus is the Son of God?" (1 John 5:5). All believers have received Christ. Thus, all believers share His victory over sin, Satan, and death. All true believers will overcome because of the persevering ministry of the Holy Spirit (Philippians 1:6).

The promise is this: all who overcome losing their first love will eat from the tree of life. When Adam sinned, he was driven out of Paradise, the Garden of Eden. Under God's judgment, he was prohibited from eating the tree of life. The truth is, this was an act of mercy on God's part; He did not allow Adam to "take also from the tree of life, and eat, and live forever" (Genesis 3:22) in a state of sin.

Only when sin is fully removed are we graciously restored to the tree of life.

In Christ, access to the tree of life is regained. Paradise lost in Genesis is Paradise regained in Revelation. So the tree of life becomes the bookends for the history of redemption revealed in the Scriptures. Satisfaction, strength, and salvation belong to the overcomer.

Recently, I must confess, I had become so busy serving the church and so preoccupied with our kids that I was neglecting my wife, Anne. My life was too busy. It was rise early, sprint to the office, study for sermons, return phone calls, dash home, play with our kids, eat dinner, help with homework, do baths, put children to bed, then collapse. Day after day. Week after week. Month after month.

I felt myself too exhausted to talk to my wife, Anne. Even when I tried to talk to her, I couldn't. The phone would ring. The door would knock. The kids would cry. The church would call. Or I was too tired.

I had to do *something*. So, taking a radical step, I bought two train tickets for just the two of us to travel to Dallas.

Alone.

My plan was to board the train and then, for seven uninterrupted hours, just be alone and talk. Just the two of us. No committee meetings. No counseling. No kids. No telephone calls. No books. No emergencies. No interruptions.

Just Anne and me.

Alone.

When we boarded the train, we had the entire passenger car to ourselves! As the train pulled out of the station, we were alone at last. Back on track with our relationship.

At first, we hardly talked. We hardly knew what to say to each other. There were no children interrupting us. We just stared at each other. Then out the window. Then back at each other.

But small talk soon became intimate talk. Here was the woman I married. It had been so long since we had had a quiet moment like this.

This was just what our relationship needed. Time alone. A second honeymoon. Just the two of us.

Do you need to do the same with *the Lord*?

Do you need to take decisive steps to be alone with Him? Has your relationship with Christ become too busy? Are you too hurried to spend time with Him? Are you too active? Too distant? Too cold? Too impersonal?

Then take decisive steps right now. *Remember* how it was when you first met Christ. *Repent* of your cold-heartedness. *Repeat* the basics—Bible study, fellowship, worship, and prayer. *Remain* on track in your fight against sin. Determine to be alone with Christ.

Have you left your first love?

He's waiting to be alone with you.

Just Him and you.

Alone.

V

WHEN PERSECUTION HITS THE FAN

Revelation 2:8–11

A LINE HAS BEEN DRAWN IN THE SAND. Sides have been taken, and war has been declared. Hell is officially in session. And the church is under attack.

With mounting hostility, the kingdom of Satan is engaging in a full-scale war against the church of Jesus Christ. The foul forces of darkness are escalating their campaign against the people of God with an unholy vengeance. Like two weather fronts colliding, a violent storm is brewing across the horizon as never before.

Witness the Hamilton Square Baptist Church in San Francisco. As church members gathered for Sunday evening worship on September 19, 1993, they knew it would be an eventful service. They just didn't know *how* eventful!

The featured guest speaker for the evening was Lou Sheldon, an outspoken opponent of pro-homosexual legislation in California. As chairman of the Traditional Values Coalition, Sheldon had played a key role in overturning a 1989 domestic partners ordinance in San Francisco.

As he came to speak, this church turned into a battleground. Two pro-homosexual newspapers had publicized Sheldon's visit, leading to a barrage of phone calls to the church all week. Militant homosexual activists promised to show up in force and threatened to disrupt the service.

And disrupt it they did. The worship service became a war zone. Like an invading army, approximately 100 rioters stormed the church ground and took complete control of the exterior property.

Angry protestors denied worshipers entrance into the church. Physical contact was used. One church member, a woman, was physically and forcibly carried away from the church's entrance by the activists.

All the while, police stood by watching. Rioters vandalized church property. The church's Christian flag was replaced by a homosexual flag. Innocent children were verbally harassed and threatened. Vile obscenities were yelled.

When the service began, angry gays (surely a contradiction in terms) pounded on the doors of the sanctuary, taunting worshipers to come outside and join them in sexual orgies. As the believers sang, the demonstrators threw eggs and rocks at the stained-glass windows. The pastor was pelted by debris and needed a police escort as he left in a church van.

Sounds like Sodom and Gomorrah.

But, folks, this is America. Today. What's next? Will this militant aggression by homosexual activists against the church continue? What other "minorities" will join their cause and level their assault upon the church? Is the final persecution of the last days now beginning?

One thing is clear. Jesus warned us it would be this way in the end times. He foretold that before His return, "They will deliver you up to tribulation, and will kill you, and you will be hated by all nations on account of My name" (Matthew 24:9).

Before His own crucifixion, Jesus told us, "If the world hates you, you know that it has hated Me before it hated you. If you were of the world, the world would love its own, but because you are not of the world, but I chose you out of the world, therefore the world hates you" (John 15:18-19). No mistaking it—the world *will* hate us.

The Apostle Paul echoed the same: "But realize this, that in the last days difficult times will come. . . . And indeed, all who desire to live godly in Christ Jesus will be persecuted" (2 Timothy 3:1, 12).

A line has been drawn in the sand. Sides have been taken. And war has been declared. Hell is in direct conflict with heaven.

The church at Smyrna knew all about this. Our Lord's second letter is addressed to the church at Smyrna—the persecuted church.

Smyrna represents every persecuted church in every age, and every persecuted believer in every cultural setting.

First, let's take a trip back to ancient Smyrna.

THE SETTING

Smyrna was easily the most beautiful city in all of Asia Minor—"the crown of Asia." It was a thriving seaport city nestled in a picturesque, natural setting. Smyrna was fronted by the coast of the Aegean Sea and flanked by a circular hill called the Pagos.

This beautiful hill, elevated above the city, was outlined with a street called "The Street of Gold." On this street were pagan temples and stately public buildings, which gave the appearance of a jeweled crown. The streets were well-paved and lined with groves of trees, enhancing its majestic beauty. Because of their symmetrical arrangement, these buildings were called "the crown of Smyrna" because from afar they looked like a necklace of jewels.

Years earlier, Alexander the Great had determined to make Smyrna the model Greek city. To many, it was. With such a noble beginning, Smyrna had blossomed into a town of advanced culture. A place where the arts, education, philosophy, and the sciences flourished. It boasted a magnificent library and a monument to Homer, who was born there. Smyrna also housed the largest public theater in Asia. Proudly, "First in Asia in beauty and size" was inscribed on their coins. Few would argue.

Located about forty miles north of Ephesus, Smyrna had a natural landlocked harbor where entire fleets could be sheltered from outside attack. This great harbor allowed it to be second only to Ephesus in exports. As a result, Smyrna was a large, flourishing center of international commerce and trade with a prosperous economy.

Notably, Smyrna had strong ties to Rome. When six cities competed for the privilege to erect a temple to Rome, Smyrna was chosen over the others. Her allegiance to Caesar was unquestioned.

Consequently, Smyrna was a thriving center for Roman emperor worship. In that day, Caesar was a god to the people. His image was carved in marble and set before the city along with burning incense. Every citizen was called upon to publicly worship and confess allegiance to Rome's ruler annually. Anyone who refused would be severely punished, immediately imprisoned, and executed by the sword.

In addition, Smyrna was a hotbed of pagan worship. Temples to Cybele, Apollo, Asclepias, Aphrodite, and Zeus were built there. Greek gods and goddesses were openly worshiped.

Nestled in the midst of this wealthy but wicked city was a little flock of believers. They had been called out of this evil system to become the church of Jesus Christ.

But Smyrna was no easy place to be a Christian. Many believers were persecuted and put to death for their faith in Christ. In fact, naming Christ in Smyrna was far more life-threatening than anywhere else in Asia.

Appropriately, the name Smyrna means "myrrh," which was a fragrant spice used to make perfume. When the bark of the flowering myrrh tree was crushed, it would release a sweet aroma. This appropriately described this church. The more these believers were crushed by the world for their faith in Christ, the more the sweet aroma of their testimony was released. Unquestionably, their faithfulness to Christ in the face of mounting opposition gave off the fragrance of Christ throughout the entire region.

If Ephesus was like New York City—the leading commercial city of the region—then Smyrna was like Atlanta—a major city known for its wealth, trade, and culture.

THE SPEAKER

Dramatically, Jesus identifies Himself to this persecuted church in a way designed to encourage and uplift their spirits. His communication was again addressed to the pastor or leader of the church. He writes:

> "And to the angel of the church in Smyrna write, 'The first and the last, who was dead, and has come to life, says this: . . .'" (Revelation 2:8).

THE ETERNAL ONE

First, Jesus is "the first and the last." This title declares His eternality. Before time existed, Jesus was already in existence. And He will be in existence after all things come to an end. From eternity past to eternity future, Jesus has been, is, and will always be the eternal and infinite One. Nothing within time presents any limitation for Him.

Jesus revealed His eternal nature to this church because in the midst of suffering, an eternal perspective is most needed. In the midst of trials, let us remember that Jesus existed before time, that He rules over time, and that He will reign for all time! What we suffer here is insignificant compared to the eternal glory that awaits us there.

THE LIVING ONE

Second, Jesus is the One *"who was dead, and has come to life."* This eternal One, who spans the eternities, *died*. How can this be?

As the eternal God, Jesus Christ invaded time and history through the womb of a virgin. He became fully human! The God-man took the form of a bond-servant and lived a sinless life. He was then falsely accused and condemned to die on a Roman cross as a common criminal. Lifted up on the cross, he hung suspended between heaven and earth. He died an ignominious death between two thieves. Yet, because He was obedient unto death, God raised Him triumphantly from the dead.

It is His victory over death that causes the church to be victorious in the face of death.

Now, *that* was a great encouragement to this struggling church. They, too, were suffering unjustly at the hands of Rome. They, too, were being obedient unto death and dying ignominiously. Just like Christ. But just like Christ, death could not hold the saints of Smyrna in its evil grasp. All martyrs will be raised triumphantly because of His eternal victory.

THE SIN

There is no rebuke for this church. No sin is corrected. No member is rebuked. While no church is perfect, in the eyes of Christ— before whom all things are open and laid bare—there is no glaring deficiency here.

It is my understanding that John gave these letters to seven messengers who crossed the Aegean Sea to embark upon a circular route to dispatch these epistles. In each community, the church would be called together. In all likelihood, all seven letters were read to each congregation.

Imagine sitting in the congregation at Smyrna and hearing this letter read. At the time when the consistent pattern called for a rebuke of sin, there was none for your church.

None.

This church found nothing but favor and approval with Christ.

THE SUFFERING

Jesus now speaks a word of comfort to this church. A persecuted church is a pure church. So, no correction is needed, just encouragement. To them, Jesus writes:

> *"I know your tribulation and your poverty (but you are rich), and the blasphemy by those who say they are Jews and are not, but are a synagogue of Satan. Do not fear what you are about to suffer. Behold, the Devil is about to cast some of you into prison, that you may be tested, and you will have tribulation ten days. Be faithful until death, and I will give you the crown of life" (Revelation 2:9-10).*

Jesus begins, "I *know* your tribulation." The word "know" (*oida*) means the kind of knowledge that comes by personal experience. It means to learn something by firsthand involvement. The word also means to appreciate, respect, or value the worthiness of a person or thing.

When Jesus says, "I *know* your tribulation," He is saying, "I *know* exactly what you're going through. I *know* because I've been there. I *know* what your tribulation feels like. I *know* what it is to be falsely accused, physically harmed, and spit upon. I *know* what it is to be beaten, mocked, and dying unjustly. I *know* what you are suffering, and I respect you greatly for it. I highly value your commitment to Me."

Jesus addresses five different levels of persecution on which this church suffered. They suffered *government persecution, economic persecution, physical persecution, religious persecution,* and *satanic persecution*—all at once! Let's examine each.

GOVERNMENT PERSECUTION

First, this church in Smyrna suffered *government persecution* under the tyranny of Rome. Jesus said, "I know your *tribulation*." He later identifies this tribulation as imprisonment by the Roman government (verse 10).

The word "tribulation" (*thlipsin*) is a very graphic word. Literally, it means to crush an object in a vise grip by tightening the screws. It pictures crushing a victim and squeezing out his life's blood. It was used of one who was mashed to death by an enormous boulder. The word also described the pain of a woman in childbirth.

In Smyrna, their life was being painfully squeezed out of them by the ironclad vise grip of the Roman government. They were being snatched out of their homes, arrested in the marketplace, and taken captive to prison. Caesar was bringing the full force of his imperial might powerfully down upon this little church. And many of them sealed their testimony with their blood.

When the church was first founded in Jerusalem, the Roman Empire was not a threat. Israel was the threat, not Rome. At the time of Christ, Rome instituted *Pax Romana*, meaning "the peace of Rome," as an expansion doctrine. As the Roman Empire conquered new territories, they were placed under *Pax Romana*.

This shrewd strategy allowed each annexed country to retain its own national leaders. But their leaders were kept only as a puppet regime. Behind the scenes, the Roman Empire placed their own man in charge. By outward appearances, nothing had changed. The people still had certain freedoms—i.e., religious practices and cultural distinctives. But in reality, the Roman Empire ruled with an iron grip.

But everything soon changed. In 67 A.D., a madman named Nero came to the throne of Rome. Deranged and paranoid, he killed his first three wives, as well as his own mother, for fear of losing his political power.

Under his insanity, the flames of persecution were ignited against the church. Nero blamed the Christians for many of his own political mistakes. This was the persecution mentioned in Peter's two epistles.

Mercifully, Nero died at a young age and Rome's persecution of the church subsided temporarily. But in 81 A.D., another insane

Roman emperor by the name of Domitian rose to power. He was even more ruthless than Nero. Suddenly a second wave of persecution against the church swept through the Roman Empire. It is to this persecution that Jesus refers in His letter to Smyrna.

As the Roman Empire expanded, it conquered many territories and countries. Consequently, there was a great diversity of languages and cultures among the peoples. How could Rome unite such divergence? How could the emperor weld together so many different nationalistic movements, some of which were conspiring to overthrow his rule?

Emperor worship became the answer. The worship of Caesar would tie the Empire together. Once a year, each citizen of Rome would appear before a bust of Caesar and publicly confess his allegiance to the deity of the emperor. For the great majority of Roman citizens, this was no problem. They already worshiped a plurality of pagan gods. What was one more god?

But for the Christians, this request was blasphemy. To worship Caesar was spiritual treason against the King of heaven. The Christians could not—and would not—cower to this idolatry. Instead of saying, "Caesar is Lord," the early believers bravely confessed, "Christ is Lord!" As a result, the church suffered painfully at the hands of the government.

One church historian writes, "To become a Christian meant the great renunciation. The joining of a despised and persecuted sect, the swimming against the tide of popular prejudice. The coming under the ban of the Roman Empire, the possibility at any moment of imprisonment and death under its most fearful forms. He that would follow Christ must count the cost and be prepared to pay the same with his liberty and life. The mere profession of Christ was a crime. For many, the name itself meant the rack, the blazing shirt of pitch, the lion, the panther, or in the case of maidens and infamy, worse than death" (H. B. Workman, *Persecution in the Early Church* [Cincinnati: Jennings and Graham, n.d.], pp. 103-104).

Such government persecution did not cease 2,000 years ago. It is still happening. In America today, we Christians are losing our religious freedom at the hands of our government. Our spiritual liberties are being stripped away almost daily as persecution from our government is increasing. Consider the examples that follow.

(Granted, some of these situations have not occurred everywhere, but they are happening in an increasing number of places.)

It is *unconstitutional* today if a student prays out loud over his lunch in school.

It is *unconstitutional* today for kindergarten students to recite, "We thank You for the flowers so sweet, we thank You for the food we eat, we thank You for the birds that sing, we thank You for everything." (You'll notice there is no mention of God in that prayer. Yet, it acknowledges one who is the Giver of all good things.)

It is *unconstitutional* today for students to arrive voluntarily early to school and to read out loud prayers that have been uttered by the chaplains in the U. S. Senate and House of Representatives and imprinted in the congressional records.

It is *unconstitutional* today for a Board of Education to use or refer to the word *God* in any of their official writings.

It is *unconstitutional* today for a kindergarten class to ask during a holiday celebration, "Whose birthday is it?"

It is *unconstitutional* today for the Ten Commandments to be hung on the walls of our schools.

It is *unconstitutional* today to introduce any bill, though it may be completely religiously neutral, if it can be ascertained that the person who introduced that bill had some religious motive.

It is *unconstitutional* for a school graduation to contain an opening prayer or a closing prayer.

In Alaska in 1987, some students were told they could not use the word "Christmas" because it contained the name Christ. Nor could it be found written in any of their notebooks by their own hand. Nor could they pass out Christmas cards to their friends in school (see the James Kennedy TV sermon/booklet, *Dawn's Early Light*).

If you think that's bad, those are just nine isolated sightings. There are currently some 500 cases just like these now proceeding through our legal systems. With every passing day, there are greater bites being taken out of our religious freedom. The noose of the government's anti-Christian agenda is being slipped around our neck, and one day, sooner than we would like to think, it is going to jerk a knot around our throats.

A couple from the church I pastor recently went to Russia to teach biblical, moral ethics to *public* schoolteachers there. I find that amazing! They had to travel halfway around the world to impart Christian values into the public school system—something they are unable to do locally in Little Rock, Arkansas. How much longer will it be before we are facing first-century-type persecution from our government?

ECONOMIC PERSECUTION

Second, there came *economic persecution* against the Smyrna church. Jesus says, "I know your tribulation and *your poverty*" (Revelation 2:9).

The word "poverty" (*ptocheian*) denotes one so poor that he has nothing at all. He is unable to find work to earn even the smallest pittance. Such a person must hold out an empty hand and hope that someone will put something into it.

That's how poor this little church was. So poor, they couldn't begin to make ends meet. Financially destitute, they didn't have a penny to their name. The reason, you ask?

Today's health and wealth movement would answer, "Because they were outside the will of God. All they had to do was name it and claim it. They were living beneath their privileges. God wanted them wealthy."

Perhaps they should have been rebuked for their poverty?

No. They suffered poverty *because* they were in the will of God. Financial prosperity is not God's will for everyone. Sometimes it costs to be a Christian. It may even cost you financially.

Remember, Smyrna was one of the most prosperous cities of its day. There was no downturn in the market there. No recession in the economy there. Business had not gone south. Everyone else in Smyrna was prospering.

Yet, these Christian businessmen were being fired from their jobs. Their stores were being broken into and looted. Their goods had been pillaged.

Why? They confessed Jesus Christ to be Lord. Not Caesar.

The closest analogy that we have is the persecution of Jews in Nazi Germany before World War II. History records that their travel was restricted. Their shops were vandalized. Their places of worship were defiled. And their property was seized. They were humiliated, dehumanized, stigmatized, slandered, harassed, and physically assaulted. They were deprived of the bare necessities of life. All this because of their religious identity.

The same economic pressure is beginning to hit Christians in America today. The price for doing business as a follower of Christ is escalating with rapid inflation.

The very week I prepared this chapter, I received phone calls from two businessmen in our church. These are two highly respected men who serve in prominent positions in highly visible companies.

The first man told me that he will be forced to resign soon. Because of his faith in Christ, the owner of the company is questioning his loyalty. He was asked, "Is your church work more important than this business? Is your Christianity more important than your career down here?" The very clear implication was, "If so, buddy, you're in the wrong place."

The second man called me with a similar story. As the Chief Operating Officer of one of the leading corporations in Little Rock, he innocently mailed out Christmas cards to his clients. These cards had his company's name on the Christmas card, along with the name of Jesus Christ. Several unbelievers were offended. This brother is now facing persecution from these clients, saying, "We're going to take this matter to the board. We are offended that you put the name of Jesus Christ on a Christmas card and mailed it to us. We will go above your head and have it stopped. And it will cost you your job!"

Both of these incidents occurred in Little Rock, Arkansas—the buckle of the Bible belt. Be sure, this will soon be playing in a town near you.

RELIGIOUS PERSECUTION

Third, Jesus identifies yet another level of persecution—*religious persecution*. Our Lord says, "I know . . . the blasphemy by those who say they are Jews and are not, but are a synagogue of Satan" (Revelation 2:9).

The noose continues to tighten. Suddenly this little church finds itself playing hardball with the religious establishment—the Jewish synagogue—and they don't have a glove. All they have is the Lord.

In Smyrna, there was a large Jewish community that was fanatically hostile against Christianity. We gain some insight into this Semitic rage when we remember the stoning of Stephen by the mob in Jerusalem (Acts 7). Jewish hatred and rage was already brewing at a fever pitch toward born-again Christians. Here in Smyrna, the Jews were even blaspheming the believers.

"Blasphemy" (*blasphemian*) means slander or speaking against. Jews were beginning to spread lies about the believers, whose reputations were being ruined. They were slandering the Christians, planting lies, and stirring up opposition. As at the crucifixion of Christ, these Jewish leaders were inciting the crowd against the Christians.

The Jews were even accusing believers of eating human flesh. Because they talked about eating Christ's body and drinking His blood (the Lord's Supper), the Jews reasoned, "These uncivilized people are nothing but barbaric cannibals."

The leaders of the synagogues also accused the Christians of gross sexual perversions. The believers talked about loving one another. They gave one another a holy kiss. They spoke of loving their brother and sister. Consequently, they were accused of incest and participating in gross sexual orgies.

The church was accused of being atheists as well. Because they would not worship Caesar, they must deny the existence of God. The church was politically disloyal because they would not bow to worship Caesar. They also accused the Christians of breaking up families because their message called for a highest allegiance to Christ.

These Jews, Jesus said, were the "synagogue of Satan." Because of their unbelief, they were instruments of the Devil, used by hell to oppose the people and programs of God. They were at Satan's disposal to carry out his will.

Similarly, the church today can expect religious persecution. Not just from the government, but from apostate churches that are no more than synagogues of Satan.

Satan goes to church just like Christians. Every Sunday the Devil says, "I've got some of my preachers I want to hear speak. I've got some of my choirs I want to hear sing. I've got some disciples with whom I want to fellowship this morning."

There are countless churches across this land that are nothing more than strongholds of Satan. They do not preach the true gospel of Christ. They deny the inerrancy of Scripture. They cast scorn on the resurrection of Jesus Christ from the dead. They promote all kinds of sexual license. They have forsaken the Word of God by ordaining homosexuals into the ministry of their churches. They condone living in gross perversion.

These "churches" are hellholes—synagogues of Satan—that will, one day soon, persecute the true church of God.

PHYSICAL PERSECUTION

Fourth, Jesus warned of a coming *physical persecution* that this church would suffer. Jesus said:

> *"Do not fear what you are about to suffer. Behold, the Devil is about to cast some of you into prison, that you may be tested, and you will have tribulation ten days. Be faithful until death, and I will give you the crown of life" (Revelation 2:10).*

It wasn't a matter of *if* they would suffer. Just *when* and *how much*. Jesus promised that more suffering was on the way. He offered no hope of deliverance. In fact, He guaranteed that the Devil was about to cast some of them into prison.

Roman prisons were ghastly places. Unlike today's prisons where you can have a private room, work on a college degree, and be fed three meals a day, nobody wanted to check into a Roman prison cell. Those imprisoned did not stay long. Either the prison authorities put you to death, or you were severely tortured and slung back onto the streets. Either way, nobody stayed long in a Roman prison.

The government was too busy to baby-sit criminals. And Rome sure didn't want to pay for feeding prisoners. Especially Christians. So, the believers were either put to death or slapped around and thrown back on the street. Believe me, no one wanted to go back for more.

How the church in Smyrna physically suffered! The Roman officials broke into their homes and arrested the believers before the startled eyes of their family. They dragged them off into Roman prisons and made public examples out of them before a watching world.

Jesus said they would "have tribulation ten days." Some Bible teachers have speculated that these ten days are symbolic of ten successive eras of Roman emperors, or ten consecutive stages of church history. Personally, I think that's more imagination than interpretation. I think they suffered for ten literal days, just as the text plainly says, in the Roman cells. Again, nobody stayed long in a Roman prison because the physical abuse was so intense. Ten days seemed like ten lifetimes.

Graciously, the Lord sets the limits to our suffering. Our tests will not last longer than we can endure. If the Lord says *ten days*, then there is no force on earth that could make it last *eleven*.

To these hated believers, Jesus said, "Be faithful until death." Some of the early believers would pay the ultimate price for being a believer in Jesus Christ by dying for their faith. In the face of such martyrdom, Jesus says, "Be faithful until death."

What would you do?

If the Roman officials came for you and said, "Caesar or Christ?" would you stand for the Lord? The answer *must* be yes. I believe that God will give us dying grace, if need be, to make such a bold confession. In the meantime, let us remain faithful to Him.

SATANIC PERSECUTION

Finally, Jesus says that they will encounter *satanic persecution*. As they live for Christ, they will find themselves attacked by "a synagogue of *Satan*." They are at war with hell itself. Ultimately, these believers did not wrestle with human flesh. Rather, their struggle was against unseen principalities, demonic powers, and evil forces in heavenly places (Ephesians 6:11-12).

Behind all persecution—whether by the government, false religion, or ungodly employers—stands Satan himself. Behind the Roman Empire stood the Evil Empire. The Devil unleashed his hellish hatred against believers by inciting unbelievers to be filled with extreme hatred toward them. All this led to their imprisonment and, ultimately, for many, to their death.

Do you see how deeply this church suffered? Simultaneously,

they suffered persecution on, not one or two, but five fronts. They were attacked politically, economically, religiously, physically, and satanically. No wonder Paul said, "All who desire to live godly in Christ Jesus will be persecuted" (2 Timothy 3:12).

Make no mistake about it. It costs to be a Christian. In some places, that cost is higher than in other places. As end-times pressures increase, persecution against the church will only increase. Around the world, churches and individuals will be called to suffer more than ever before.

Again, notice that there is no rebuke for this church. Out of the seven churches, Jesus rebukes five of them. But for two churches, there is no criticism. The other church that escapes rebuke is Philadelphia. Not coincidentally, that was another persecuted church. The lesson is very clear. *Persecution purifies the church!*

Think about it. If the world is persecuting you, do you really think you would love the world? Would worldliness be a temptation if the world was attacking you? Of course not!

If you were locked up in a Roman dungeon, in solitary confinement, would you leave your first love? Not likely. Whom else would you talk to? Would you neglect prayer when you're sitting, bruised and bloody, in a Roman prison cell? No way!

If the world was attacking you, would you have trouble loving other believers? Not when Christians are the only people who accept you. You're just glad to be with somebody that's not going to kill you. There were no problems with false teachers in the church at Smyrna. Not when it was being attacked by the Roman Empire. The persecuted church will always be a pure church.

Let's face it, we don't handle prosperity well. Only in crassly materialistic America can you turn on the radio and hear prosperity preachers pampering the unbridled lusts of carnal people, saying, "God will make you rich. God will make you wealthy if you just have faith and trust God."

The greatest blessing that could ever happen to the cause of Christ might be for the American church to be persecuted. Someone has said, "The problem with Christians these days is no one wants to kill them anymore." Such persecution would melt us down to the bare essentials of what it means to be a genuine follower of Christ.

What counsel did Jesus have for this suffering church? Just two reminders. "Do not fear" (verse 9), and "Be faithful" (verse 10). We might wish there was more hope to it than this. But that's all He says. "Do not fear . . . Be faithful."

Why would Jesus say this? It should be obvious. Some of them were fearful and in danger of weakening. Why else would He say, "Do not fear" and "Be faithful"?

The way not to fear is to replace your fear with a greater fear. One fear must displace another. The way not to fear man is to fear God. Reverence to God overpowers our fears of men. We must hold God in highest respect and awe. Fear God and you won't fear men!

Fearing God begins with a high view of God. Cultivate an understanding of His awesome holiness. Bow before His absolute sovereignty. Kneel before His blazing righteousness. Being consumed with the grandeur of God causes us to fear Him.

One step further. Jesus says, "Be faithful unto death, and I will give you the crown of life." In the face of death, the believers were to keep on being faithful. They must not shrink back from dying for Christ's name. Not every Christian is called to be a martyr. But every disciple must be willing to make such a sacrifice.

Our willingness to die for Christ is the ultimate proof of our loyalty to Him. We are not ready to live until we are ready to die.

Believers who die for their faith in Christ will be richly rewarded. A "crown of life" awaits them after death. This "crown" (*stephanos*) pictures the garland of victory—a laurel wreath—that was awarded to the winner of the athletic games of the day. Their faithfulness unto death would bring the victor's crown from the hand of Christ.

Here is strong motivation to remain faithful to Christ—even unto death. A special crown, the martyr's crown, awaits all those who pay the ultimate price to be a follower of Jesus Christ.

That's what God is asking you and me to do. "Do not fear" and "Be faithful."

THE SUMMONS

Despite the world's fierce persecution, overcomers will have a great victory over the world. Jesus concludes with a call to hear and heed this message. So, He writes:

"He who has an ear, let him hear what the Spirit says to the churches"
(Revelation 2:11a).

Every ear must tune in to what Jesus has said. These are weighty words to be obeyed. Jesus says, "Pay very close attention. Take these truths into your heart."

Matthew Henry writes, "The surest evidence of our love to Christ is obedience to the laws of Christ . . . love is the root, obedience is the fruit."

The story is told of an eleventh-century German king, King Henry III, who grew tired of court life and the pressures of being a monarch. So, he applied to a monastery to be accepted for a life of contemplation.

The religious superior of the monastery, Friar Richard, is reported to have said, "Your Majesty, do you understand that the pledge here is one of obedience? That will be hard because you have been a king."

King Henry replied, "I understand. The rest of my life, I will be obedient to you, as Christ leads you."

"Then I will tell you what to do," said Friar Richard. "Go back to your throne and serve faithfully in the place where God has placed you."

When King Henry III died, it was said, "The king learned to rule by being obedient."

Like King Henry, we must be obedient to what the Spirit says to do. Whether you are an accountant, a teacher, a mother, a father, or whatever, you must serve God where He has placed you.

THE SUCCESS

It is to the one who hears and obeys what the Spirit is saying that Jesus makes a staggering promise.

"He who overcomes shall not be hurt by the second death" (Revelation 2:11b).

Remember, all true believers are overcomers (1 John 5:5). Jesus promises that overcomers shall not be hurt by the second death.

The first death is a *physical* death—the separation of the soul from the body. The second death is a *spiritual* death—the separation of the soul from eternal life. Spiritual death results in the eternal lake of fire. Not annihilation, but conscious, unending punishment (Revelation 20:10).

True believers will never experience this second death. Never! Someone has said that we are either born once to die twice or born twice to die once. Christians can face the first death without fear because the second death has no power over us. We can look physical death square in the eye—even while suffering martyrdom for Christ—knowing that death will simply usher us into Christ's presence.

This message to Smyrna is a call to be fully dedicated to Jesus Christ, even in the face of persecution and death. As the world grows darker, the church must shine brighter. Now is the time to stand up for Jesus Christ.

No matter what the cost!

One man stands out as a visual reminder to us of this truth.

In the second century, the pastor of the church in Smyrna was a man by the name of Polycarp. He was the bishop of the church at Smyrna. History and tradition say that Polycarp himself knew the Apostle John and had heard from his very lips the words, "Remain faithful until death."

In A.D. 155, at the age of 86, Polycarp was summoned before the Roman proconsul at Smyrna. The proconsul demanded that Polycarp take an oath renouncing Christ and claim allegiance to Caesar. Polycarp refused. He said, "Eighty-six years have I served the Lord Jesus. He has been faithful to me. How can I be faithless to Him and blaspheme the name of my Savior?"

"Swear by the name of Caesar," the proconsul insisted, "or I will have you torn and fed to the animals."

"Then hand me over to the beasts," said Polycarp. "You will not change my heart. I tell you plainly that I am a Christian even until death."

Enraged, the proconsul sent a messenger out into the city of Smyrna to proclaim that Bishop Polycarp had committed high treason against Rome by admitting to being a Christian.

The messenger gathered a blood-thirsty mob together in the arena of Smyrna, where intense anti-Christian hatred had poisoned the city. There, the enraged crowd built a pyre of boards and planks while they clamored that Polycarp be handed over to them.

Polycarp was delivered to the mob, which had brought hammers and nails to nail the bishop's hands and feet to the stakes that were being set afire.

Polycarp then uttered those famous words, "Put away those nails and let them be. The One who gives me strength to endure the flames will give me strength not to flinch at the stake. You threaten me with a fire that burns for a short time and is quickly quenched. For you do not know the fire that awaits the wicked and the judgment to come and an everlasting punishment. Why are you waiting? Come do what you will to me."

As the wood was piled around his feet and ignited, Polycarp turned his eyes toward heaven and said, "O Lord, God Almighty, Father of the blessed and beloved Son, Jesus Christ, I thank You for giving me this day and this hour that I might be numbered among the martyrs to share the cup of Jesus and to rise again to life eternal." He bowed his head and said, "Amen" as the fires consumed him at the stake.

Polycarp was faithful until death. He feared not the world. He feared God. And great is his reward in heaven.

May it be so with you and me. When persecution hits the fan, let us not fear the world—but God and God alone.

No matter what the cost!

VI

LIVING AT HELL'S HEADQUARTERS

Revelation 2:12–17

A SPECIAL EDITION OF TIME MAGAZINE, entitled "Beyond the Year 2000: What to Expect in the Next Millennium," recently gave us a glimpse into the near future. As *Time's* editors and sociologists projected into the future, the view was not a pretty one.

What will America look like in the year 2000? What will our culture look like? Where are we headed as a society? What will our lifestyle be? Here is the picture being portrayed for America by the turn of the century:

First, *multiple marriages*. "The family as we know it will soon die," they predicted. It will be nothing more than an interesting anomaly—a mere blip in human history. We thought of it as "normal," but we were wrong. Replacing it will be marriages, or what will soon be "serial monogamy."

Second, *widespread divorce*. "Divorce will be so common as to be considered normal. Some marriage contracts will have sunset clauses—to automatically terminate at a given date."

Third, *women living together*. "Many women will live with other women, much like the 'Golden Girls' are depicted on the television sitcom."

Fourth, *multiple parents*. "Children will live with a bewildering array of relatives—mothers, fathers, multiple stepmothers, multiple stepfathers, stepbrothers, stepsisters, grandparents, former grand-parents, etc."

Fifth, *incest*. "The taboo against incest will weaken. The fractured family will consist of relatives, non-relatives and former relatives, breaking down the obsolete prohibition against intimacies at home."

Sixth, *childlessness*. "The trend toward childlessness will acceler-ate." There will be more older people and fewer children than ever before.

Seventh, *child abuse*. "Children will be routinely victimized and will be bounced from home to home as families splinter and reform and splinter and reform. Many children will have no one to care for them. Boys and girls will roam the streets much like they did in Charles Dickens' London, or as they still do today in Brazil."

Eighth, *sexual explosion*. "Pediatricians will teach children about the use of condoms at the time of their vaccinations against disease."

Ninth, *atheism*. "Theology, the study of God and the Bible, will soon die. School children of tomorrow will have no knowledge of spiritual matters, nor even any interest in this topic."

Tenth, *feminism*. "The triumph of feminist religion will cause many to shun references to God in personal masculine terms (no more 'Lord' or 'Heavenly Father')."

Finally, *abortion*. "Forced abortion, such as China imposes on its women, will be necessary in nations with exploding populations." Representative Pat Schroeder spelled out the ideal: "The most important goal for the 21st Century is family planning for everyone."

The bottom line? Here's what these socialists see in the future: "An even more radical approach may evolve. It is reasonable to ask whether there will be a family at all. Given the propensity for divorce, the growing number of adults who choose to remain single, the declining popularity of having children, and the evaporation of the time families spend together, another way may eventually emerge. It may be quicker and more efficient to dispense with fam-ily-based reproduction. Society could then produce its future gen-erations in institutions that might resemble state-supported baby hatcheries."

Not a pretty picture. Begin with multiple marriages, divorce, and lesbianism. Throw in incest, childlessness, and child abuse. Add sex-ual promiscuity, feminism, and abortion. Stir well with atheism.

That's the world in which we will find ourselves. So says *Time* Magazine. And those editors and sociologists may be right, which is cause for concern. Undoubtedly, we have already entered a post-Christian era in America. An era in which the culture is becoming increasingly hostile to biblical values and morality.

We, the church, will find ourselves ministering in an increasingly godless society. We are now living at hell's headquarters. We have set up church at the gates of hell.

How should we then live? What should be the church's strategy amid such culture wars? What counsel does Christ have to offer?

Now, more than ever, we must hear what Jesus said to a little church in Asia Minor in the city of Pergamum. It was a church that lived at hell's headquarters. They occupied the same neighborhood as the Devil. They served under the dark shadow of Satan's throne.

Pergamum wasn't an easy place in which to live. Yet, that's where God planted this church. In this letter, Christ calls them to remain true amid such a hellish environment.

THE SETTING

Located about 55 miles north of Smyrna and 20 miles from the Aegean Sea, Pergamum was the capital city of the Roman province of Asia Minor. It was the place from which the Roman Empire ruled this part of the world. Politically, to control Pergamum was to control Asia Minor.

In 29 B.C., the civic leaders of Pergamum proudly built the first known temple in Asia to Caesar. Emperor worship had its strongest grip here. In other cities, the citizens gave public testimony to Caesar's deity once a year. But here in Pergamum, imperial idolatry was a daily lifestyle. A pinch of incense burned in worship of the emperor was an everyday occurrence.

Here, the people regularly testified to their allegiance to Caesar. It was no problem to serve other gods, just as long as one served Caesar. One could say, "Zeus is Lord" as long as he also said, "Caesar is Lord." No problem. Or one could say, "Apollos is Lord, *and* Caesar is Lord."

But the rub for the early believers came precisely here. Christians could not serve two gods. They could not deny their Lord by saying, "Caesar is Lord." Blasphemy! Participating in the imperial cult would be high treason against heaven's King. As a result, believers in Pergamum were being put to death for their faith in Christ.

A 1,000-foot-high hill overlooked the city and was covered with pagan temples, shrines, and altars. Zeus, Athena, Dionysius, and Asclepias each had temples built here.

A huge altar to Zeus, the greatest of all the Greek deities, had been built here in the form of a throne. Many feel that "Satan's throne" in this letter refers to this. Regardless, at that time it was the most famous pagan altar in the world.

So deeply entrenched in idolatry was Pergamum that they had their own god named Asclepias, the god of healing. Worshipers would come into the temple of Asclepias to be healed. Snakes roamed wild throughout the temple. Worshipers were encouraged to lay down on the floor and allow these snakes to crawl over their body. Healing power was believed to be in the touch of these vipers. In fact, the symbol of the medical profession—a twisted serpent—represents this god of healing, Asclepias.

The city was noted for its well-known library. Parchment—a new writing material made from animal skins—was first developed here. In fact, the name *Pergamum* means "parchment." The library eventually grew to 200,000 volumes before it was shipped to Egypt by Cleopatra.

That's where this church found itself. Living at hell's headquarters. Serving next to Satan's throne. Here is divine instruction that is most timely for our generation given the drift of our culture toward greater godlessness. This letter is definitely relevant.

If Ephesus was like New York City, a bustling, cosmopolitan seaport city of commerce and international impact—and if Smyrna was like Atlanta, a growing metropolis soon becoming a major city—then Pergamum was like Washington, D. C., the capital seat of government for that part of the world.

THE SPEAKER

Like the other letters, Jesus first reveals Himself to this congregation. The divine call is extended from Christ, through the angel, or pastor, to this congregation. That's the role of any pastor. Simply to be the conduit for God's Word. The message is never to originate with himself, but with Christ. The pastor is the delivery boy of this letter, not the editor. So, Jesus, the Chief Correspondent, says:

> *"And to the angel of the church in Pergamum write: 'The One who has the sharp two-edged sword says this: . . .'"* *(Revelation 2:12).*

In Roman culture, a sword was the symbol of *power and authority*. In that day, Rome had the power of the sword, meaning in its hand was the power of life and death. Caesar had the power of final judgment.

The sword meant the power of capital punishment. It represented the power of the government to put criminals to death. Appropriately, Paul wrote to the church in Rome that the governing "authority . . . does not bear the sword for nothing; for it is a minister of God, an avenger who brings wrath upon the one who practices evil" (Romans 13:1-4).

There was no confusing the issue. The sword meant the authority to take human life at will. As such, Rome raised the sword with absolute sovereignty over the people. Whatever Caesar determined became the law of the land. And he backed it up with the sword.

As such, Jesus is pictured holding a sharp, two-edged sword. This denotes His judicial authority to pronounce and execute judgment. With sword drawn, Jesus Christ is pictured as the Divine Warrior defeating His enemies in battle, pronouncing judgment upon them. He is the unrivaled Lord of His church, with power over life and death. His word is final. His law is binding. His rule is absolute.

Why a "two-edged sword"? Because it cuts both ways. Christ has power over life and death. He possesses authority to bless and to curse, to save and to damn.

Why does Jesus reveal Himself *this* way to *this* church? As this two-edged sword cuts both ways, two reasons stand out.

The first is *positive*. This church is already suffering persecution under the sword of Rome. No doubt intimidation and fear were gaining footholds in their hearts. They must be reminded that an authority far stronger than Rome was being wielded over their heads. Despite Rome's fear tactics, Christ is still the One ultimately in control of all world powers.

The second is *negative*. As we shall learn, this church was tolerating false teachers. They needed to be reminded that there is an unchanging standard—God's Word—by which God measures all truth. They must defend sound doctrine. If they don't remain true to the faith, they will face severe discipline from the hand of Christ Himself.

This is a sobering picture of Christ. Not of the Good Shepherd. Nor of the meek and mild Messiah. Although He is both, here we see Christ with a "sharp two-edged sword" drawn, ready to devour His enemies.

The church today is infatuated with the image of a Lamb, but not a Lion. We have lost our fear of God as a consuming fire.

Every church must see this Christ. It is by Him that we rise or fall.

THE STRENGTHS

Jesus now commends this church for their steadfastness. Jesus writes:

> "I know where you dwell, where Satan's throne is; and you hold fast My name and did not deny My faith even in the days of Antipas My witness, My faithful one, who was killed among you, where Satan dwells" (Revelation 2:13).

This is a sympathetic word of encouragement. Again, Jesus is saying, "I *know* exactly where you're living. I *know* what you're going through. I've been there. And I highly respect and value your faith in Me."

Jesus Christ *knew* what living at hell's headquarters meant. From the time of His birth, Satan began nipping at His heels. After forty days and forty nights in the wilderness, Jesus battled Satan head to head. All the artillery of hell was leveled at Christ. All the way to the cross, the Devil opposed and stirred up persecution against Christ.

Interestingly, Jesus defeated the Devil in the wilderness with a sharp, two-edged sword—God's Word. When He was tempted, He thrust the sword into Satan, "*It is written*, 'Man shall not eat by bread alone.'" Again, He jabbed, "*It is written*, 'Thou shalt not put the Lord thy God to a foolish test.'" Once more, Jesus drew the sword and said, "*It is written*, 'Thou shalt have no other gods before Me.'" Jesus rammed Satan through with the Word of God. For the church at Pergamum, appropriating Christ's words would bring the same victory over Satan.

These believers in Pergamum lived "where Satan's throne is . . . where Satan dwells." It was his regional headquarters. A satanic stronghold. A beachhead for evil. Satan visited other towns, but he lived in Pergamum.

The devil is not omnipresent. He can only be in one place at one time. So, he might spend the night in Laodicea, Sardis, or Ephesus. But he lived in Pergamum!

"Satan's throne" means the place where his evil authority is most exercised. It is where he exerts great power and influence. "Dwell" means to move into a house and live there permanently. This was Satan's neighborhood!

Why was Pergamum "Satan's throne"?

First, it was—as stated earlier—the center of worship of Asclepias, the snake god. Here in Pergamum, they worshiped in a great pagan temple with many snakes crawling inside the temple. Of course, all such superstitious idolatry was demonic. Satan, the serpent, was fueling the worship of this snake god.

Second, Pergamum was—as we noted earlier—the regional center of emperor worship. It was the first city in Asia to have a temple devoted to the divine Augustus. A special priesthood was also devoted to this imperial cult. Compared to other cities, Caesar adoration was most intense here.

Jesus commends them that they held fast His name without wavering. These believers remained strong in their personal loyalty to Christ as Lord and refused to worship Caesar. Despite adverse pressures, they remained faithful and true. They stood strong for God's standard of truth amid the moral decline of the day.

One man in particular—named Antipas—was especially bold in his faith. His name, Antipas, means "against all," and that's precisely what he did. In his defense of the faith, he stood against all. This one man—probably the pastor of the church—refused to yield to the "political correctness" of the day. Apparently, he was the leader of the

Christian resistance to local pressure to compromise their loyalty to Christ.

We are not told, specifically, what the issue was. He probably stood up to the government, because only Rome had the power of capital punishment. In a day of moral apostasy and a decline in decency, Antipas stood against Rome's totalitarian demands for absolute allegiance.

Jesus said Antipas is "My faithful one." What greater tribute could be given? God has called us to be *faithful* in our witness, not successful. We are to leave the results with Him.

Did it cost Antipas? It cost him dearly. He was "killed among you, where Satan dwells." Whatever the issue was, it was obviously a hill worth dying on. Antipas, this faithful pastor, gave his life for the cause of right in a day of wrong.

As Tertullian said, "The blood of martyrs is the seed of the church." If so, then Antipas' faith has yielded a bumper crop for centuries to come. The world looks at a martyr's death and says, "What a loss." But God says, "What gain!" May his tribe increase.

What hills do you believe are worth dying on? What issues are worth giving your life for? In what do you believe so strongly that you would be willing to lay down your life?

A wise Christian knows which battles are worth fighting. A faithful Christian will do so.

THE SIN

So, is this a perfect church? Hardly. Despite their steadfastness, sin slipped in undetected. Their real danger was not with persecution. It was perversion within the church. If Satan can't defeat a church, he'll join it. Notice the deadly threat from within. Jesus continues:

> *"But I have a few things against you, because you have there some who hold the teaching of Balaam, who kept teaching Balak to put a stumbling block before the sons of Israel, to eat things sacrificed to idols, and to commit acts of immorality. Thus, you also have some who in the same way hold the teaching of the Nicolaitans" (Revelation 2:14-15).*

There's that little phrase again—"But I have a few things against you." It sends a chill up my spine. It grabs me by the lapels and jerks me up to attention.

Within the church, there was a small group that was teaching compromise with the world. Their carnality was threatening to harm the whole fellowship. A little leaven infiltrates the whole lump. Here in Pergamum was a small group entangled in the teaching of Balaam.

Christ's complaint is not directed to the small group teaching this heresy. His rebuke is against the majority in the church who tolerated the teaching of Balaam.

Who was Balaam? What did he teach?

Balaam was an Old Testament prophet, a Gentile who knew God. He was called to be a mouthpiece for God but often spoke for the Devil.

During the time of Israel's wilderness wanderings, God's chosen people defeated the Ammonites, and Moab looked surely to be the next to fall. When Balak, the King of Moab, received a report that the Israelites were advancing his way, he knew there was no way his army could defeat Israel.

In desperation, Balak called on Balaam for help. The Moabite king said, "I've got an assignment for you. I want you to curse these people. And I'll make it worth your while."

Yielding to the temptation, Balaam sold his gift for profit. Three separate times he tried to curse the people of God. But each time only blessings—not cursings—came out. Try as he may, Balaam could not curse the people of God.

So, Balaam became frustrated. He tried to serve God and money at the same time, but he couldn't serve two masters. Under mounting pressure, Balaam devised an ingenious plan. If he couldn't curse them, his only hope was to get *God* to do so. So, Balaam hatched an insidious plot.

The "profit prophet" would teach Balak to put a stumbling block before the sons of Israel. He instructed the corrupt king to place sensuous women before the marching Israelite army. Let these beautiful women tempt and lure God's people into sin. God would judge them for their disobedience.

Balak did as Balaam suggested, placing enticing Moabite women before the Israelite men. The sons of Israel were no match for this temptation. They wilted under the seductive power and decided to party with these pagan women. Before they knew it, they laid down with dogs and got up with the Devil's fleas. Soon they went to church with these heathen women and worshiped their idols. They even brought sacrifices to their pagan gods and ate meat offered to idols in pagan ceremonies.

Not to be confused with eating meat offered *to* idols (1 Corinthians 8), these men were eating meat *with* idols. They were worshiping idols *in* the Moabite pagan temples. In these temples were sensuous prostitutes who lured the men of Israel into further immoralities. The result was devastating. Israel fell into this terrible sin, and God went to war against them. He slew *24,000* Israelite men!

What Balaam couldn't do to harm Israel, sin did. The stumbling block was devastating! A stumbling block (*skandalon*) is a trap set with a bait. When the bait is touched—*boom!*—the trap is triggered, and it closes shut on its victim. That's what sin is like. It looks alluring, but when touched, it captures its unsuspecting prey.

The teaching of Balaam is to compromise with the world. It is the mixing of holy things with unholy things. It is having one foot in the church and one in the world. Trying to play both ends into the middle.

This small group in the church at Pergamum was threatening to destroy the whole church. Only one link has to break before the whole chain is useless. Only one cancer cell needs to become malignant and the whole body will soon suffer.

So it is in the church. A little leaven affects the whole lump. A small pocket of sin will infect the whole body. It must be dealt with. Now!

In addition, Jesus addresses another dangerous sin lurking in the church. There was a second group teaching false doctrine—the Nicolaitans. They taught a destructive license very similar to the teaching of Balaam. Different bottles, same poison.

Tradition says Nicholas was one of the first leaders appointed in the church (Acts 6:5). In time he apostatized, teaching that a believer has moral license to live however he or she wants. He tried to reach a compromise between the Christian life and the cultural customs of the Greek-Roman society.

In reality, the teaching of the Nicolaitans combined Christian ideals with immorality and idolatry. The result was a devastating heresy that threatened the very existence of the church. They espoused a perverted liberty of God's grace called antinomianism—the belief that none of God's moral laws are binding on the Christian today.

Restated, the teaching of Balaam and the Nicolaitans encouraged believers to engage in idolatry and immorality in their Christian lives.

What is idolatry? It is anything or anyone in your life that is more important to you than God. It is *loving* anything more than God. *Fearing* anything more than God. *Serving* anything more than God. *Desiring* anything more than God. It is anything that comes between you and God.

An idol can be a statue carved out of marble. But it can also be a checkbook made out of paper. A car made out of steel. A boat made out of fiberglass. A house made out of wood.

An idol can be a degree framed and mounted. A cause joined and served. A talent mastered and employed. A physique developed and tanned.

It is anything—or anyone—that occupies first place in your life instead of Jesus Christ.

John warns, "Do not love the world, nor the things in the world. If any one loves the world, the love of the Father is not in him" (1 John 2:15). James cautions, "Do you not know that friendship with the world is hostility toward God? Therefore whoever wishes to be a friend of the world makes himself an enemy of God" (James 4:4).

To each of us, the Bible says, "Little children, guard yourselves from idols" (1 John 5:21).

Do you think we have idolatrous teaching in our churches today? Surely no one's teaching that kind of stuff, are they?

Wrong. To this day, the teaching of Balaam is present in the church. Turn on the television and you can hear these so-called "teachers" today who pamper our flesh and tempt us to want more and more of this world. Of course, all this to the exclusion of godliness and contentment with what you have.

Charles Colson points this out in his book *The Body*. Colson writes:

While settling into our Los Angeles hotel room for the night, we flipped on the television and scanned the channels waiting for something to catch our eye. It did. A man and a woman were seated on an overstuffed sofa in the middle of a grand, gaudy set. A huge, stained-glass window shimmered in the light next to a portrait of Jesus on black velvet. Large palms spilled out of every corner. The white and gold baby grand was a showstopper.

But it was really the two sitting on the couch that got our attention. His salt and pepper hair combed back in neat waves looked like it might be held in place by epoxy cement. His dark eyes and moustache would have made him seem as sinister as a wild west villain if it weren't for the charming foil provided by his mate.

She was a southern belle done by Frederick's of Hollywood, with a fuchsia, ruffled dress, and huge, silvery blonde hair. She sat primly, holding her Bible, alternating adoring glances at her husband with arch-eyed eyebrows and nods to the studio audience, apparently coaching them to adore him, too. Her smile remained as fixed as his hair. Perhaps relaxing it would have cracked her make-up.

But it wasn't just the absurd scenery and costumes that captivated us. It was the message of this Christian—yes, Christian—program. "You can have perfect peace and joy and happiness and prosperity," the host said. "God wants no one to be poor. God wants no one to be deprived. Just ask and you will receive in abundance. Yes, abundance, abundance, abundance. God wants you to prosper. God wants you to be rich. You can have it all."

My friend, *that* is the teaching of Balaam!

The Word of God says, "Seek first His kingdom, and His righteousness; and all these things shall be added to you" (Matthew 6:33). "Set your mind on the things *above*, not on the things that are on *earth*" (Colossians 3:2).

But the teaching of Balaam—today called the "word of faith" movement, the "health and wealth" gospel, or the "name it, claim it" movement—teaches just the opposite. It teaches, "Seek first the kingdom of *this world*, and spiritual things will be added to you."

Such heresy feeds our greed. It arouses materialism, stimulates worldliness, and pampers covetousness.

Multiplied millions of dollars are being pumped into ministries like this. In reality, they are stroking the flesh of those who send in their money, telling their duped followers that they can have all that this world has to offer. Now. That's exactly what Balaam taught.

But not just idolatry. Let me go one step further. The teaching of Balaam is also promoting *immorality in the church*!

Wait a minute. Surely, no church is doing that! If anyone is going to stand up for purity, fidelity, and virginity, it is the church. Right?

Wrong. Just as in the church at Pergamum, there are teachers today lowering the standard of purity to its basest form. Tragically, there is teaching today—in the church, no less—that promotes sexual compromise.

Many churches and denominations are sanctioning the ordination of homosexuals into the ministry. They are even establishing homosexual churches. Other churches are approving divorces without biblical grounds. They are also sanctioning remarriages without biblical grounds. Still others are quickly reinstating immoral leaders back into their pulpits. They are condoning people living together. Many are approving abortion as a birth control measure. Most are failing to discipline church members who are sexually unfaithful to their spouses. They are tolerating pornography in the private lives of their leadership.

Get it straight. *This* is the immoral teaching of Balaam!

The word *immorality* (*porneia*) is an all-encompassing, generic word that includes all forms of sexual perversions. Adultery. Premarital sex. Homosexuality. Lesbianism. Bestiality. Pornography. Common-law living together. Transvestism. You name it. The whole stinking mess.

The church must not—and cannot—condone these perversions. Instead, we must wield the sharp, two-edged sword and remove them from the church.

Recently I was talking to a man about his relationship to the Lord. He was under great personal pressure. Years ago, he divorced his wife and abandoned his kids. Compounding his guilt, he was now shacked up with another woman.

This man wept like a baby and prayed with me to receive

Christ. After we prayed, I told him, "Now, you understand that you're going to have to stop living with this woman and go back and marry your wife. Or you need to marry this woman that you're now living with. But you cannot continue to live with a woman who is not your wife."

He came back to church the next Sunday. After the worship service, we went back into my office. He was as giggly as a teenager. Obviously he had some good news to tell me.

He said, "Steve, I've moved out."

I got excited with him. Until I got the rest of the story. He then added, "I've moved out now, and I'm in the bedroom next to hers."

"Time out," I said. "That's not good enough. The Bible has a standard. 'Thou shalt not commit adultery.' I don't care if you're sleeping in her bed or she's in your bed. What you're doing is wrong."

This man hasn't come back. But the fact remains: the church cannot condone immorality. He has gone back to his previous church that accommodates this kind of lifestyle.

The Bible hasn't changed one bit. God says, "You shall *not* commit adultery" (Exodus 20:14). "*Flee* immorality" (1 Corinthians 6:18). "This is the will of God, your *sanctification*" (1 Thessalonians 4:3). "Let the marriage bed be *undefiled*" (Hebrews 13:4). "Do *not* let *immorality* or *any impurity* . . . even be named among you" (Ephesians 5:3).

The teaching of Balaam has a devastating effect upon a church. One drop of poison pollutes the entire glass of water. So, Jesus says, "There is a small group in your church that is teaching compromise with the world. Deal with it."

What about *you*? Are you living a double life? Are you unfaithful to your spouse? Are you involved with anyone else? Are you even emotionally involved with someone else?

Men, do you stay pure when on a business trip? Are you renting dirty, filthy videos? Are you reading pornographic magazines? Are you having an affair? Are you even *thinking* about having an affair?

Women, are you fantasizing about someone else? Are you watching the "soaps" during the day? If so, you are flirting with disaster.

Singles, are you keeping yourselves pure? Are you guarding your virginity?

"It is time for judgment to begin with the household of God"
(1 Peter 4:17).

THE SOLUTION

After making the proper diagnosis, the Great Physician now prescribes the only cure—open-heart surgery. Jesus says:

> *"Repent therefore; or else I am coming to you quickly, and I will make war*
> *against them with the sword of My mouth" (Revelation 2:16).*

Repentance calls for a change of mind with respect to sin.
Likewise, there must be a change of heart and will. One's entire life
must dramatically change. That's repentance.

Jesus says, "Get right now. Turn your life around. Stop seeking
the world. Reverse your field. Reroute your life. Head in a new
direction."

These are strong words. But serious danger awaits them if they
continue in their idolatry and immorality. Serious danger calls for
serious action.

Jesus doesn't say, "That's okay. I've got unlimited grace and
unending forgiveness, so it doesn't matter how you live."

No way. Jesus says, "Repent therefore; or else I am coming to
you quickly, and I will make war against them with the sword of My
mouth." His coming here is not the *Rapture*. He's talking about a
rupture.

This is a threat. A warning to heed. This refers not to His
Second Coming, but to a special coming in judgment to this particular church. Such a judgment fell to Balaam (Numbers 22:23, 31;
25:5; 31:8). And such a severe discipline will come against the
Balaamites and Nicolaitans in this church.

The church must deal with its sin, or Jesus will come and deal
with the church. Either the church will discipline its sinning members, or Jesus will come and make war with His sword.

No church wants to be on the short end of that sword. True to
His word, Jesus will fight against any church that accommodates sin
within its membership. He will war against those congregations who
are lenient toward immorality and idolatry.

This ought to be a wake-up call!

Being tolerant of these doctrinal deviations makes the entire church, especially the leadership, as guilty as those who teach and hold to this false doctrine. The entire church is called upon here to "repent," either of holding to this heresy or of allowing it to spread.

With a spirit of gentleness, the church must go to members of their body who are entrapped in sin, the goal being to restore them to holiness (Galatians 6:1-2). First, one goes; then, two or three witnesses; then tell it to the church and commission the entire church to go (Matthew 18:15-17). If such a person in sin will not listen and repent, then put him or her out of the church.

The message is clear. Idolatry and immorality is not to be tolerated in the church. Either the church will deal with sin, or Jesus will. But it *will* be dealt with.

THE SUMMONS

Jesus, the wonderful Counselor, concludes with a closing word of comfort:

> *"He who has an ear, let him hear what the Spirit says to the churches"* (Revelation 2:17a).

Again, Jesus issues the admonition to hear what He has said. The church must take to heart this warning. To hear and fail to act is not to hear at all.

Jesus says, "Why do you call Me, 'Lord, Lord,' and do not do what I say?" (Luke 6:46). We must listen to what the Holy Spirit is saying and follow His counsel.

THE SUCCESS

What if the church does repent? What if it will overcome its compromise with sin? What if idolatry and immorality are dealt with? What hope is there?

Again, Jesus provides us with a foretaste of heaven in order to motivate us to obey His word to the church. He holds out the future glory of heaven as an incentive for present commitment.

*"To him who overcomes, to him I will give some of the hidden manna,
and I will give him a white stone, and a new name written on the stone
which no one knows but he who receives it" (Revelation 2:17b).*

To the one who overcomes these sins, great blessing is promised.
It matters how we act upon our Lord's message. To the one who
repents, Jesus promises hidden manna, a white stone, and a new
name.

HIDDEN MANNA

First, Jesus promises *hidden manna*. In the Old Testament, manna was
the heavenly food that God provided for His people in the wilderness. It was manna that the Israelites were eating when they encoun-
tered Balaam. In contrast to the food offered to idols, God provided
holy food from above.

Christ is the true manna, the living bread that comes down from
above (John 6:35). This speaks of our fellowship with Him. Christ
invited the church at Laodicea to "dine" with Him (Revelation 3:20).
Dining is a picture of close intimate fellowship with another person.
Here, believers are promised sweet communion with Christ forever.

Why is it called "hidden?" Because it is a sweet communion that
the world does not know—it can only be known by faith. Jesus offers
spiritual bread, unseen to the natural eye, as opposed to the bread
that can be seen and eaten.

A WHITE STONE

Second, He promises *a white stone*. This could mean one of two
things.

First, in ancient times, a white stone referred to the judicial practice of registering a vote of acquittal (compare Acts 26:10). In a courtroom, a judge would render his verdict by placing a white or black
pebble in an urn. Black meant condemned. White meant acquitted.
If we will confess our sin and repent, then Christ will register a verdict of acquittal. Confession brings forgiveness. Repentance reverses
the court's decision of certain condemnation.

Another understanding, and the more probable explanation,
arises from another use of white stones in this first-century culture.

White stones were often given as a symbol of appreciation and acceptance, or specifically as a means of admission to a special event. Christ promises all true believers that in overcoming, they will be rewarded with eternal acceptance and admission into His presence.

A NEW NAME

Third, overcomers receive *a new name*. A new name indicates a new identity. A new standing. A new beginning. It reflects a believer's new status in Christ.

This new name is unknown to others. No one else can possibly know fully what Christ means to me, or to you. The relationship between Christ and the believer is so intimate and personal that the full depths of such a spiritual experience cannot be known by anyone else.

Do you see how these three all fit together? One day each of us will be accepted (white stone) into the presence of Christ to enjoy sweet fellowship (hidden manna) according to our new status in Christ (new name).

What do these images remind you of in our present culture?

Think of the analogy of marriage. A young couple stands at the altar. The glow on the face of the bride reflects a profound anticipation. She comes to the altar with a white stone on her finger to receive a new name and identity and to enter into a richer, deeper relationship with the one whom she loves.

God has chosen to use this common marriage experience as a picture of our future glory with Him. A wedding feast awaits us (Revelation 19:1-10) at which time we—His bride—will be fully accepted into a more intimate relationship with Him. Just as a bride receives a new name, so shall we who overcome.

Like the bride at the altar, our hearts should be filled with anticipation of the glorious consummation of our relationship with Christ. This anticipation should motivate us to spiritual purity and fidelity today.

But while we wait, the bride of Christ lives at the front steps of hell's headquarters. Surrounded by the forces of evil, she must combat Satan and the hordes of hell. The battle roars all around us.

We, the church, cannot ignore the spiritual conflict that rages on every hand. Nor can we afford to be safely isolated within the four walls of the church. We must be the church and penetrate our culture, which is under siege by Satan.

In 1917, the Russian Orthodox Church met in Petrograd. The agenda? The church's leadership deliberated in deep debate and heated argument over—are you ready for this?—the color of their liturgical garb.

All the while, just a few blocks away the godless Communist revolution was breaking out and was spilling Russian blood in the streets. While the church met, hell's headquarters—just blocks away—commenced the takeover of a nation.

Doesn't this picture the church in America today? While Satan and his legions are pushing a cultural revolution all across the land, we are deliberating behind cloistered walls, where we trivialize the essentials and debate the minutiae.

If we are to be the church, we must be faithful to Christ and so penetrate our world.

No matter where we live, hell's headquarters are but a few blocks away. The danger is great today. Greater than it's ever been. And the forces of hell are closer than ever before.

But the opportunity for the church today has never been greater either. Especially while we live at hell's headquarters.

VII

DEVIL WITH A BLUE DRESS ON

Revelation 2:18–29

IF THERE IS A WATCHWORD that describes the American mind-set today, it is the word tolerance. We Americans worship at the shrine of tolerance. In the shaping of public opinion and the forging of national policy, we esteem the broadmindedness which says any and all values, if sincerely held, are equally valid.

There are no absolutes today. The only absolute is that there are no absolutes. We tolerate everything except intolerance.

Tolerance. Webster defines the word as "the allowable deviation from a standard; sympathy or indulgence for beliefs or practices differing or conflicting with one's own."

That, in a nutshell, is America. A broadmindedness as wide as America itself. An openness that embraces almost *anything* morally, politically, or educationally.

George Gallup, America's pollster, says that 67 percent of Americans today believe that there is no such thing as absolute truth. In other words, right and wrong varies from situation to situation. It may be wrong for me, but right for you.

Translated, if homosexuality is right for you, that's fine. If it's not right for you, well, that's fine, too. Whatever works for you is right for you. If it feels good, do it.

The consequences are terrifying.

Newsweek, in its December 7, 1992, issue, published an article entitled, "What Traditional Family?" The article referred to traditional values as a "myth" that never existed in American life. Interpreted, "we're rewriting history in order to be politically correct."

In the same issue, *Newsweek* carried an article entitled, "Losing Our Moral Umbrella." In this report, the writer argues that America never had a common moral consensus. The article says, "There is no such thing as the Judeo-Christian tradition. It's a secular myth favored by people who are not really believers themselves."

In America today, there is a growing and emerging belief that there is no absolute truth. No standard of right and wrong. The result is tolerance of any and every belief in our culture.

Francis Schaeffer has properly described our modern-day mindset when he said, "Modern man has both feet firmly planted in mid-air."

Charles Colson has said, "Our moral senses have been permanently neutered. We have undergone a moral lobotomy." The sin that used to slink down the back alley now struts down Main Street. Like ancient Israel, we have become a people who have forgotten how to blush. Nothing shocks us. Tragically, we have become desensitized toward sin.

The flickering flame of our national conscience is all but extinguished. All forms of abnormal and immoral behavior, once considered unthinkable, are now embraced. In the name of tolerance, we have now opened the floodgates to embrace every form of wickedness.

We have recently witnessed Exhibit A of the new American spirit. In an unprecedented move, newly-elected President Bill Clinton has moved to remove restrictions allowing homosexuals into the military. At no point in national discussion is there intelligent debate about moral absolutes. All we want is tolerance. We are quick to sacrifice sacred virtue on the secular altar of tolerance.

If we continue to reject absolutism, the belief in fixed moral standards, we are headed for doom. The Bible, the sharp, two-edged sword, is now being replaced with the Devil's pitchfork. Morality is now defined with a Burger King philosophy—"Have it *your* way— rather than by heaven's King. An absolute standard of right and wrong is fast becoming a dusty page of ancient history.

Who is to say which abnormal perversion will be accepted next? Will it be bestiality? How about polygamy? Or child pornography? Will it be transvestism? What "alternative lifestyle" will be next to be embraced?

As the church, we are beginning to feel the tightening noose of the world around us. If we are not careful, we will soon be choked to death by public consensus.

Paul warns us, "Do not be conformed to this world, but be transformed by the renewing of your mind, that you may prove what the will of God is, that which is good and acceptable and perfect" (Romans 12:2).

This was the tightening squeeze that the church at Thyatira felt—the crunch of remaining intolerant in a tolerant society. Sadly, the world was influencing this congregation more than they were influencing the world. In reality, this church was being duped into believing that they could live like the world and still be the church.

Jesus must forcibly address this church. He must tell them that He is intolerant of that which they tolerate. There was a woman in their congregation, Jezebel, who was dressed to kill. She was a devil with a blue dress on.

It is no different today. The church is still being confronted with devils wearing blue dresses, who seek to lure and seduce the church. As the American culture becomes more pervasively evil, we will increasingly feel the pressure of the world to adopt their "politically correct" agenda of tolerance. Nevertheless, God's standard of truth never changes. "The grass withers, the flower fades away, but the word of our God stands forever" (Isaiah 40:8).

Let's look now at this letter to the church at Thyatira.

THE SETTING

Of the seven cities, Thyatira was the smallest. Located about 30 miles southeast of Pergamum, Thyatira was a small industrial center on the highway between Pergamum and Laodicea. It was out of the way. The least known. The most obscure.

Thyatira was a "blue-collar" working town known for its numerous trade guilds. Carpenters, dyers, merchants, cloth makers, and other trade workers had organized fraternal guilds, much like our labor unions today. These trade guilds were so strongly union-ized that it was near impossible to make a living in Thyatira without being a "card-carrying" member.

In addition, each guild had its own pagan deity. After hours, the members were expected to attend the guild festivals. These included a feast of eating food offered to their idol and plunging into the vilest sexual orgies. All this was like combining a labor union with a trade guild and a college fraternity.

Unlike the other cities, Thyatira wasn't the religious center of any pagan worship. There were no large, imposing pagan temples here, although pagan deities did exist. Apollo, the son of Zeus, was the divine guardian of the city. Likewise, emperor worship was not a great threat here. Pressure from Rome to impose emperor worship in Thyatira was negligible compared to the nearby Pergamum.

Thyatira was a sentinel military town. It was originally settled to intercept any foreign armies approaching Pergamum. Before an invading foe could threaten the capital city, Pergamum, it had to defeat Thyatira first.

This was Thyatira. A small town. Hard-working. Blue-collar. Country. Rough, tough, and coarse.

If Ephesus was like New York—if Smyrna was like Atlanta—if Pergamum was like Washington, D. C.—then Thyatira was like Cleveland or Detroit. It was a hard-working labor town with all the roughness that goes with it.

It was in this difficult setting that the church at Thyatira existed. God never has to have the circumstances just right to build His church. Often it is in the least likely places where God chooses to do His greatest work.

THE SPEAKER

Again, Jesus begins with a sobering self-identification of Himself. The kind intended to get their attention. Here's how He reveals Himself to this church.

> "And to the angel of the church in Thyatira write: 'The Son of God, who has eyes like a flame of fire, and His feet are like burnished bronze, says: . . .'" (Revelation 2:18).

ABSOLUTE DEITY

First, Jesus identifies Himself as "the Son of God." This title declares Christ's absolute Deity. He is co-equal and co-eternal with God the Father. As the Son, His special relationship with the Father establishes the authority of His judgments. He is divinely commissioned to execute God's purpose on the earth, especially in the church.

PENETRATING GAZE

Second, He has "eyes like a flame of fire." With omniscient gaze, Jesus is able to see into the secret places of our hearts. He has the supernatural ability to search out and probe our inner man. His holy intelligence pierces our façades. He unmasks our disguises. He uncovers our pretensions.

Jesus sees what no one else can see. He audits our core attitudes. He evaluates our inner motivations. He weighs our driving ambitions. He observes our secret thoughts. Everything is laid bare before Him. Nothing is hidden from His glowing eyes. Nothing.

This divine gaze is like "a flame of fire." Everything yields to fire. Fire consumes all that it touches. So it is with Christ's white-hot, holy gaze. Everything in the church is exposed by his holy intelligence. Nothing escapes.

PURGING JUDGMENT

Third, Jesus has "feet like burnished bronze." With blazing feet, He stands strong in judgment over this church. He purges out and tramples down all sin. He detects and judges it all. His verdicts cannot be overturned.

Why does Jesus reveal Himself *this* way to *this* church? Because they have become tolerant of sin. Christ must reassert His authority with this church—more so than with the three previous churches. In no uncertain terms, Christ will not tolerate a church married to the world.

The church must see again this portrait of Christ as Judge. When a church starts tolerating sin, they must understand that Christ, the Good Shepherd, is also their holy Judge. This letter is a serious wake-up call to any church flirting with the world.

THE STRENGTHS

Christ first commends the church at Thyatira. There are definite virtues for which Christ can praise them. Our Lord writes:

> *"I know your deeds, and your love and faith and service and perseverance, and that your deeds of late are greater than at first" (Revelation 2:19).*

This church had a lot going for it. Love, faith, service, and perseverance marked their congregation. These four virtues are actually two couplets. Their love led to their service, and their faith produced perseverance.

LOVE AND SERVICE

Of the seven churches, this is the only one singled out for their *love*. While love for Christ was decreasing in Ephesus, it was increasing in Thyatira. This church remained deeply in love with Christ. In a day of callous indifference, their devotion to Christ grew stronger and stronger.

Love for Christ was Number One in this church. It was the driving force of the membership.

Many years ago Thomas K. Beecher once substituted for his famous brother, Henry Ward Beecher, at the Plymouth Church in Brooklyn, New York.

Many curiosity-seekers had come to hear the renowned Henry Beecher. But when Thomas Beecher appeared in the pulpit instead, some people got up and started for the doors. They were sadly disappointed to miss the opportunity to hear the famed orator speak.

Sensing their disappointment because he was substituting for his brother, Thomas raised his hand for silence. He then announced, "All those who came here this morning to worship Henry Ward Beecher may withdraw from the church. All who came to worship God may remain."

Love for Christ—not for any man—must always be central in the church. That definitely was the case in Thyatira. Jesus commended them for their affection for Christ.

This fellowship remained deeply in love with Christ. They loved

God with a holy passion. In a day of callous indifference, their devotion to Christ grew stronger and stronger.

Their love for God produced *service*. Love must be our divine motivation to serve others. They were constantly reaching out to minister to the needs of others. They gave themselves tirelessly to one another.

D. L. Moody once said, "The measure of a man is not how many servants he has, but how many servants he serves." If so, this church was large in stature because their service was great.

A businessman once asked Lorne Sanny, then president of the Navigators, how he could know when he had a servantlike attitude. The answer was, "By how you act when you are treated like one."

Are you a servant? In what ministry context do you consistently serve? Whom do you sacrificially serve? How do you respond when you are treated like a servant?

FAITH AND PERSEVERANCE

Also, *faith* marked this congregation. They trusted God to guide and provide. They relied upon Him to meet their needs. They were committed to following Christ.

Martin Luther said, "Faith is a living, daring confidence in God's grace, so sure and certain that a man could stake his life on it a thousand times."

Their faith produced *perseverance*. Perseverance (*hupomone*) is a steadfast endurance that bears up under great stress and mounting pressures. Their faith kept them faithful to complete the task to which Christ had called them.

Faith and works are as mysterious as the sun and sunlight. Faith is the sun; good works are its visible rays.

What's more, their love, service, faith, and perseverance were increasing. Jesus noted, "Your deeds of late are greater than at first." By no means stagnant, this church was growing in each of these areas.

So, what could possibly be wrong with a flock like this? Isn't love all you need?

THE SIN

When Oliver Cromwell sat for the official portrait that would portray his appearance to future generations, he instructed the artist to paint him just as he saw him. He wanted no flattery. In Cromwell's words, he instructed the artist to paint him "warts and all."

As Jesus paints the picture of this church, He does so warts and all. He must now expose this church's sin if the picture is to be accurate.

> *"But I have this against you, that you tolerate the woman Jezebel, who calls herself a prophetess, and she teaches and leads My bond-servants astray, so that they commit acts of immorality and eat things sacrificed to idols. And I gave her time to repent; and she does not want to repent of her immorality" (Revelation 2:20-21).*

Shifting gears, Jesus says, "But I have this against you." Unlike the praise that just preceded, He now brings a scathing rebuke of this church. Speaking directly to the problem, Jesus indicts them for tolerating a woman in their church whom He calls "Jezebel." Their sin is, they tolerate her false teaching in the church.

This church had love, but no sound doctrine. Ephesus was just the opposite. They had sound doctrine, but no love. A church will usually be polarized in one or the other direction. Either they will have full heads and empty hearts, or full hearts and empty heads. Either polarization is deadly.

Balance is the key in any church. God demands both love and sound doctrine. We must "speak the truth in love" (Ephesians 4:15).

Doctrine and love are like the two chemical ingredients of salt. Interestingly, salt is composed of two poisons: sodium and chloride. If we ingest one without the other, we would die. But if we combine them together properly, we have sodium chloride, which is common table salt. It gives flavor to food and life and health to our bodies.

So, too, must doctrine and love be inseparably bound together. One without the other leads to a deadly imbalance. Separately, they can be deadly. But combined, they provide health to the body of Christ. The church at Thyatira had gotten out of balance. They had all love, but no doctrine. The result was devastating.

Their lack of sound doctrine made this church easy prey for the false teaching of a woman in their congregation whom Jesus calls "Jezebel." Let's meet Jezebel.

I doubt this woman's real name was "Jezebel." After all, Jezebel was the most evil woman in the Old Testament. It is inconceivable that any parents would have named their daughter Jezebel. That would be like naming your son Judas. I have three sons—Andrew, James, and John. But no Judas.

In reality, there was a "Jezebel-like" woman in the church. A prominent, influential woman, behind the scenes, controlling the life of the church. Like Jezebel of old, she was the evil power behind the throne. Or at least behind the pulpit.

So, Jesus nicknamed her Jezebel. Christ often gave people names that reflected their character. He did so with Simon, renaming him Peter. Our Lord does the same here with this woman, renaming her Jezebel.

What was this Jezebel doing? In order to understand her sin, we need to understand Jezebel in the Old Testament. This infamous woman was the daughter of the king of Sidon, a people famous for Baal worship. The worship of Baal, the pagan fertility god, included the grossest sexual immoralities imaginable. The temples of Baal were filled with temple prostitutes, both male and female, and the basest sexual practices.

Jezebel married Ahab, the king of the northern kingdom of Israel. When she moved in, she brought her pagan idolatry with her. In remaining loyal to Baal, she introduced Baal worship to Israel and financially supported 850 false prophets of Baal.

Eventually, Jezebel became the evil power behind her husband's throne. Although Ahab was the king, Jezebel ran the country through her husband. She was the puppeteer behind the scenes, pulling the strings and setting the agenda in Israel.

In truth, she was a devil with a blue dress on.

Ahab had a nice "presidential" smile that gave him favor with the nation's policymakers. But inwardly he was the most evil king Israel had ever had. This was no "odd couple." They were equally yoked.

Israel's "first lady" had Naboth the prophet killed. Then she had the rest of the prophets of God killed. She promoted her idolatry and immorality throughout the land. She attempted to murder the prophet Elijah after his famous encounter with 450 false prophets of Baal.

This she-devil with a blue dress on wore the pants in the family. She was the sinister power behind Ahab's scepter. Ruthless. Godless.

Calculating. Scheming. Power-mad. A seducer of people. While Ahab was the figurehead, she was the sovereign head.

There's a valuable lesson to be learned here. We in America must be careful whom we elect into political office. Behind a "presidential" smile may be a devil with a blue dress on.

But back to Thyatira.

There was a woman in this church just like Jezebel. Her husband may have been an elder or a deacon. He may have been a prominent businessman. We don't know. But one thing is clear: she ran the church. As the church's power broker, she pulled the strings behind the scenes. Through her influence as a teacher, she was leading astray many of the members. While her students were taking notes, she was directly influencing them to "commit acts of immorality and eat things sacrificed to idols."

With a touch of sarcasm, Jesus said that she "calls herself a prophetess." God didn't call her this. She was a self-appointed mouthpiece for God. Not everyone who says they speak for God speaks for God. Not everyone who has Reverend before their name is reverent. Not everyone who talks *about* God speaks *for* God.

Through her teaching, this Jezebel was encouraging her class to engage in immorality and idolatry. Here's how it was happening.

Thyatira was a blue-collar town. A hard-working town with a strong work ethic. As we mentioned earlier, there were trade associations which were like the merger of three different institutions—a labor union, a trade guild, and a college fraternity. The men would work together all day, then party together all night. In order to have a decent job in Thyatira, it was necessary to be a member of a trade guild. If you were a carpenter, you had to join the carpenter's guild. If you were a plumber, a member of the plumber's guild. And so on.

These guilds combined the worst of both worlds. They mixed the peer pressure of a labor union with the gross immorality of a fraternity. After working all day, the "brothers" put their tools aside and gathered together to party. They would bring out their little pagan gods and start their idolatry. Prostitutes were involved as well. The orgies that followed the feasts dedicated to pagan gods were well-known happenings. It was *Animal House* with a work ethic.

William Barclay writes, "These guilds met frequently and they met for a common meal. Such a meal was, at least in part, a religious ceremony. It would probably meet in a heathen temple and it would certainly begin with a libation to the gods and the meal itself would largely consist of meat offered to idols. The official position of the church meant that a Christian could not attend such a meal."

The Christian workers were put in a very difficult position. Obviously, it was wrong to participate in this wickedness, and yet, because of the economic pressures, they would be out of work if they didn't. Some of the Christians were weakening, rationalizing that it was acceptable in order to provide for their families. A "lesser of two evils" reasoning.

Worse, this Jezebel was teaching them to join the unions. Her teaching was probably, "An idol is nothing. Go ahead and get involved in the guild. Participating in a meal to an idol won't hurt you. God will overlook it."

In other words, business is business. She said, "This is a great opportunity to build bridges toward the world. Participate in their drunken parties and before you know it, they will be visiting church."

This false prophetess was actually teaching "the deep things of Satan" (verse 24). She taught that you can't overcome evil until you know all about it and even try it. Unfortunately, many in the church were buying into this and were being led astray.

Furthermore, Jesus said, "I gave her time to repent" (verse 21). God had already rebuked her for this false teaching. Whether through His Word, her conscience, the pastor, or an itinerant evangelist, God had confronted her. It probably came from the Apostle John himself because of his authoritative position among the churches of Asia.

Despite having ample time to repent, she *refused*. "She does not want to repent of her immorality," Jesus said. She likes her sin. She will not give it up.

She was a devil with a blue dress on.

We have Jezebels in church today. Their weak husbands sit on boards while they pull their strings and control the politics of the church. These are devils with blue dresses on who drain the church of its power.

While we are on the subject, Jezebels are not confined to the church. We have them in the government today, as well. After electing certain officials, we think that we have elected the man for whom we voted. But in reality we have elected the evil woman behind his office. Such women misguide our country through the control of their husbands. They are devils with blue dresses on.

THE SUFFERING

Sin, unconfessed and unrepented, always brings suffering. There is an unbreakable law in God's moral universe of sowing and reaping. We always reap what we sow. If we sow sin, we will surely reap suffering. That's the law of the harvest. Consequently, Jesus promised:

> *"Behold, I will cast her upon a bed of sickness, and those who commit adultery with her into great tribulation, unless they repent of her deeds. And I will kill her children with pestilence; and all the churches will know that I am He who searches the minds and hearts; and I will give to each one of you according to your deeds" (Revelation 2:22-23).*

This Jezebel-like woman had been conducting her business in bed. Apparently, she had been seducing her disciples. There was a group in the church that was continually engaged in adultery with her.

Jesus warned of the inevitable result: "I will cast her upon a bed of sickness." She will be punished in the very place where she sinned.

What was her sickness? Hardly the flu or a cold. Jesus identifies it as a fatal disease—"I will kill her children with pestilence." The word "pestilence" means disease or germs. In this case, it is life-threatening. Jesus is saying, "If you continue in your sexual perversions, I'm going to cast you into a bed of disease and germs."

This is a clear reference to sexually transmitted diseases. Gonorrhea and syphilis were common in the ancient world. Sow to the flesh, reap to the flesh.

Sexual promiscuity has a payday someday. Every kick has a kickback. Solomon wrote, "Can a man take fire in his bosom, and his clothes not be burned?" (Proverbs 6:27). Play with fire and you'll get burned!

Unquestionably, we are seeing the same consequences to our sin

in America today. Is AIDS the judgment of God upon a promiscu-
ous society? I believe so.

Jesus promised to throw Jezebel's followers into the same "bed
of sickness." This refers not to her physical children, but to her students under her spiritual influence—her disciples, if you will. Those
who absorb her teaching will be killed by it. She was a devil with a
blue dress on. Dressed to kill.

Tragically, we are seeing this in the church today. The immorality of the world has invaded the church. In some cases, there is little, if any, difference between the world and the church. The lines
have become blurred, and the church's witness is suffering greatly.

The church must be a pure and holy bride. A chaste virgin.
Betrothed to one Husband. We must be wholly holy.

Jesus promised, "I will kill her children with pestilence." The
question is raised, "Would God kill a believer? Would He put to
death one of His own children?" According to the Bible, yes. Jesus
is saying, "If *you* won't discipline her and her followers, then *I* will.
It will be a discipline unto death."

There can come a time in the life of a Christian when God
chooses to take his or her life. A believer can go too far into sin and
commit a sin unto death. John writes, "There is a sin leading to
death" (1 John 5:16; cf. 1 Corinthians 11:29-30). Certainly, they were
not too sinful to go to heaven. Just too sinful to stay on earth.

Jesus tells us why He takes such action. He does this so that "all
the churches will know that I am He who searches the minds and
hearts." He exercises severe discipline so that the other churches will
know that He is serious about holiness in the church. This situation
was so bad that it was widely known in the other cities. So it had to
be dealt with decisively.

In other words, Jesus says, "I've got to discipline Thyatira
because Ephesus is watching. I can't let this go unchecked because
Smyrna is watching. I must deal with this sin because Pergamum is
watching. If I don't judge Thyatira, then Ephesus, Smyrna, and
Pergamum will begin to live like this."

Recently I was sitting at McDonald's, reading a book and working on a sermon. I don't know why, but any time I go to study in a
public place like that, I'm a magnet for trouble. Especially for somebody with at least five little children under the age of five.

Sure enough, a dear, precious lady with five little kids sat down in the booth right next to me.

At first, the kids were all relatively calm, eating their hamburgers and devouring their french fries. Then suddenly one of these children pulled out the world's most deadly weapon—a packet of ketchup. Now armed and dangerous, this little terrorist started squirting ketchup at his siblings. Ketchup was flying helter-skelter! I watched it spray all over the wall next to me.

In self-defense, I got up and retreated to the other side of my booth. I figured I could at least dodge what was coming at me if I could just see it.

The mom gently whispered to her little terrorist, "Now, honey, stop that!"

This only motivated him more. He pulled out some more ketchup and escalated the war. Now ketchup was going everywhere, and his siblings were ready to retaliate.

The mother repeated, "Now, honey, please, stop that!"

No response. He just kept reloading and firing away. This major offensive lured the others to enter the war. Soon a major food fight broke out.

Frustrated, she pleaded, "Oh, please stop that. Son, stop that! Mommy's going to have to do something about that."

I wanted to stand up and shout, "Listen, son, stop it!"

But I didn't. I just sat tight, ready to prepare my own packet of ketchup.

As this scene continued to unfold, an interesting phenomenon was occurring. The longer this mother just *talked* but didn't discipline, the more the other kids got into the act. Eventually, all five were chucking french fries at one another. All the while, this precious mom just smiled and whispered, "Stop, children."

I wanted to say, "Mom, you don't understand. If you don't discipline one, you're going to have all five acting wild." Truth is, if she had disciplined the first child, the other four would have never gotten involved. Disciplining one will keep the others in line.

That's precisely what Jesus is saying here.

"I'm going to discipline you, Thyatira," He says, "because Ephesus is watching. And because Smyrna is watching. And because Pergamum is watching. I can't let your sin go unchecked. If I don't come and discipline you—even to the point of killing a few members—there's no telling what sin will occur in the other churches."

There are too many spiritually immature adults in churches today who need to be disciplined. Too many food fights are going unchecked in churches today. And that's sending the wrong signal to other believers that immorality is okay.

God is serious about our holiness. Each of us must examine our hearts for sin. Too often we pamper and tolerate our little pet sins when, instead, we ought to deal with them ruthlessly. Jesus said, "If your right eye makes you stumble, tear it out. . . . If your right hand makes you stumble, cut it off" (Matthew 5:29-30).

I'd say that's a serious call to personal holiness.

THE SOLUTION

Jesus now speaks to the rest—the faithful remnant—who have not become entangled in this evil woman's teaching. In many compromising churches, there is a faithful remnant that remains true to the Lord. Such was the case in Thyatira. Here is our Lord's counsel to the faithful believers there. He addresses the rest who were not a part of Ms. Jezebel's class.

> *"But I say to you, the rest who are in Thyatira, who do not hold this teaching, who have not known the deep things of Satan, as they call them —I place no other burden on you" (Revelation 2:24).*

Ms. Jezebel called her teaching "the deep things of God." But sarcastically, Jesus called it instead "the deep things of *Satan*." She insisted that in order to better resist sin and the Devil, one has to first experience it. Sound familiar? Wasn't that Satan's original temptation of Eve? He came as a serpent to Eve and whispered, "Listen, you need to eat from the tree of knowledge of good and evil. If you know about evil, then your eyes will be opened, and you'll be like God. You've got to experience sin if you're ever going to resist it."

That's the Devil's lie. God says, "Abhor what is evil; cleave to what is good" (Romans 12:9). Get a Ph. D. in goodness; be ignorant of evil.

It's a travesty that school and government officials are insisting that we educate our little children in certain sexual sins. At a certain age, such education is needed. But not in kindergarten. Instead, our young children need to be innocent of that evil, not to be trained professionals.

Jesus places no *other* burden upon these believers. What burden does He give them? The burden of having to bear with Ms. Jezebel until something is done with her. In other words, "Just deal with her. That's all I want you to do. Just deal with her."

In the meantime, "hold fast" (verse 25) to your purity. Hold on to your virginity. Hold on to your fidelity. Hold on to your integrity. Hold on to the truth. Don't let go of your grip on it. Hang on! Because when you lose those things, you can never get them back. Don't let go of what is right!

Flee temptation, and leave no forwarding address.

THE SUCCESS

Jesus concludes this letter with a much-needed word of comfort. After such a sobering wake-up call, they were, no doubt, ready for a word of hope. So, here is Christ's promise to those who will overcome Ms. Jezebel's seductive influence:

> *"And he who overcomes, and he who keeps My deeds until the end, to him I will give authority over the nations; and he shall rule them with a rod of iron, as the vessels of the potter are broken to pieces, as I also have received authority from My Father; and I will give him the morning star"* (Revelation 2:26-28).

PRIVILEGED AUTHORITY

First, Jesus promises to give overcomers authority over the nations. In this promise, Jesus quotes Psalm 2:8-9. That is a messianic psalm looking ahead to the second coming of Christ to destroy God's enemies. When Christ returns to this planet, He will establish His earthly kingdom. In that day, we will rule and reign with Him. We will share in His coming judgment upon the earth.

Many churches hold annual missions conferences to promote the worldwide enterprise of the gospel. One popular missions speaker has stated that at several such conferences he has noticed banners declaring, "Ask of Me, and I will surely give the nations as Thy inheritance" (Psalm 2:8).

This is a flagrant misunderstanding of this text. The psalm goes on to state the nature of this inheritance. It is an inheritance of judgment! The Heir, Jesus Christ, executes judgment: "Thou shalt break them with a rod of iron, Thou shalt shatter them like earthenware" (Psalm 2:9).

In that day, Christ will rule the unbelieving nations with a rod of iron, smashing them like a potter breaks a hardened clay pot. The vessels of a potter are made of clay—dried, cooked, hardened, and brittle. When struck, such earthen containers are easily shattered into hundreds of pieces with a single, sharp blow. This graphically pictures the collapse of God's enemies at the return of Christ.

With a royal scepter like a rod of iron, Jesus will crush sinners into small pieces with fierce wrath. The lost will be severely destroyed. R. C. Sproul says, "Modern man is betting his life that this is it and that there is no judgment." That, my friend, is a bad bet!

The overcomer is promised the privilege of authority in governing the earth and in judging the nations with Christ.

PROMISED ACCESS

Second, Christ promises to give believers "the morning star." You know who the Morning Star is—Jesus Christ Himself. Jesus says, "I am . . . the bright morning star" (Revelation 22:16). What's the point?

The morning star does not appear until immediately before the sunrise. When the night is the darkest, that's when the morning star appears. And when it does appear, it is the brightest star in the sky.

So it will be at Christ's return. Jesus will come as the bright morning star at the rapture of the church. That's when history will be approaching its darkest hour. As the present day becomes darker, let us lift up our heads and look up for Jesus—the bright Morning Star. Let us be "looking for the blessed hope and the appearing of the glory of our great God and Savior, Christ Jesus" (Titus 2:13).

THE SUMMONS

Finally, Jesus says:

"He who has an ear, let him hear what the Spirit says to the churches"
(Revelation 2:29).

We must pay careful attention to what Jesus says. To hear and not to obey is not to hear at all. What is the Spirit saying in this letter? That we cannot tolerate sin in the church, or in our lives. It must be dealt with severely.

Recently I was visiting family in Gastonia, North Carolina. On Saturday afternoon, my brother-in-law lined up a golf game for us with two other men.

On the first tee, we introduced ourselves, and it didn't dawn on my brother-in-law to tell them that I was a preacher. That was a mistake. Beginning on the first hole, the language coming from these two was pretty bad. They used words that would curl the ears of a sailor.

After the first few holes, their golf got worse and worse, while ours got better and better. Soon, we were beating them rather handily. After every shot they made, they cursed—"What a 'blank' shot," or "That's the worst 'blanking' shot I ever hit in my life." Their vulgar language went from bad to worse.

Finally, we finished the front nine, having beaten them out of a Coke. As we made our way to the tenth tee, one of the gentlemen, hoping to win back his Coke, bellyached, "We're going to double the 'blankety-blank' bet. You 'blankety-blanks' are beating us too bad."

Looking up with a sheepish grin, my brother-in-law deadpanned, "Well, I don't know whether that would be a good idea. You don't want to give more of your money to the preacher, do you?"

"Preacher?"

The air became deathly silent. Both of their jaws hit the ground.

"Who's a preacher?" one of them snapped.

"Well, Steve here is a preacher in Little Rock, Arkansas."

Those two men froze. They rolled their eyes over at me like I was a ghost. Then they stared back at each other.

"Why didn't you tell us . . ."

They apologized profusely to me for cursing and taking God's name in vain. Then they assured me that this wasn't their normal way of talking. I responded, "It wasn't *my* name that you were taking in vain. And you won't be standing before *me* on Judgment Day."

For the next few holes, I could see them talking to each other, replaying all that they had said. If they missed a shot, their language changed dramatically. They would say, "Oh, shucks!" Or, "Horsefeathers!" Or, "Golly!"

When we got to the fifteenth green, these men tried to cut their losses. Which only made it worse. The first said, "You know, Steve, I'm the Chairman of the Elders over at First Church." (I'll withhold the name to protect the guilty.)

The other said, "Yeah, I sing in the choir and teach Sunday school there. I'm real active on the Board of Deacons. In fact, we're singing Handel's *Messiah* tonight."

"Well, I can see that I need to come to your church and hold a revival real soon," I replied.

Frankly, I think that Christ needs to come to a lot of our churches. Our Lord needs to come and hold revival services soon. Especially where church leaders are tolerating sin in their lives. We have too many Jezebels in our churches. God is absolutely intolerant of sin in the church. So should we be, too! If the church isn't pure, it has nothing to say to the world.

What about your church?

What about you?

Are you tolerating sin in your life? We must launch a holy war against sin. If we don't, He will.

And let the purging begin with me.

VIII

CHURCH OF THE LIVING DEAD

Revelation 3:1–6

A DEAD CHURCH?

Sounds like an oxymoron. You know what an oxymoron is, don't you? It's two words that are seemingly contradictory, but are joined together. It's two opposites that are attached that seem incongruous.

Like black light. Jumbo shrimp. Dead live oak. Ill health. Army intelligence. Rap music. Good casserole. Freezer burn. Postal service. Old news. Pretty ugly. These are tandems which shouldn't fit together, but they do.

But, a *dead church*?

That has to be the ultimate oxymoron. The greatest of all contradictions. How can you have a dead church? Especially if the living Lord indwells it? How can a congregation be dead if the life of God pulsates through that body?

Tragically, many churches *are* dead! Like the rotting carcass of Lazarus, these church bodies have the foul stench of death upon them. They have the appearance of life, but they are, in actuality, dead.

Their sanctuary is a morgue with a steeple. They are congregations of corpses. They have undertakers for ushers. Embalmers for elders. And morticians for ministers. Their pastor graduated from the Cemetery.

The choir director is the local coroner. They sing "Embalmed in Gilead." You might say their worship is a bit stiff.

At the Rapture, they will be the first churches taken because the Bible says, "The dead in Christ shall rise first." They drive to church in one long line with their headlights on.

Whenever someone joins their membership, the church office immediately notifies the next of kin. The church van is a black hearse. Their church sign is a tombstone.

The Divine Coroner pronounces such churches dead.

Maybe you heard about the little boy who walked out of the church sanctuary one Sunday. Out in the lobby was an engraved plaque listing all the members of the church who had died in military service. The little boy asked his father, "Dad, what's that?"

The dad replied, "That's for the members who died in the Service."

To which the little boy asked, "Which service did they die in, Dad? The morning or the evening service?"

Maybe you've attended a dead church like that. The sermon was *dead*. The worship was *dead*. The fellowship was *dead*. They lost vital signs years ago. Worse yet, maybe you *attend* a church like that *now*. Worse, maybe *your* spiritual life is like that. Dead. Dormant. Dull. You once were excited about your faith in Christ, but now your heart is lifeless. You once lived *on* the cutting edge, but now you've gone *over* the edge.

The fact is, you're *dead*! Not unconverted. Saved, but uncommitted, undisciplined, unfaithful.

There was a time when your heart once shed tears in church. But no longer. Dead noses smell no roses. A "Do Not Disturb" sign hangs around your neck. No one else can see it, but God can. You used to study God's Word daily, and your communion with Him was vital. But no longer.

This was the church at Sardis. A church with a great reputation. A storied history in the past. But now? There is no life. No dynamic. No pulse. No heartbeat. As Jesus addresses this church, He has something very poignant to say to every church today.

THE SETTING

Sardis had once been one of the greatest cities of the ancient world. Founded some seven centuries before the coming of Christ, it had a long and rich history. As the capital of the ancient kingdom of Lydia, it had been one of the wealthiest cities of the world. The city of Sardis was synonymous with wealth, prosperity, and success.

The city lay about 50 miles east of Ephesus at the junction of five main roads, making it a center for trade. The city was known for its manufacture of woolen garments. The main religion in the city was the worship of Artemis, one of the nature cults that was founded on the belief of death and rebirth.

Sardis was located on an almost inaccessible plateau. The acropolis of Sardis was some 1,500 feet above the valley floor. As such, the city was thought to be an impregnable fortress against military assault.

This security bred a smug self-sufficiency. The citizens thought they were invincible against invading armies. So, they ceased positioning their watchmen on the tower. But Cyrus, king of the Medo-Persians, captured Sardis by scaling a secret path up the cliff below. Once conquered, the city fell into a downward spiral from which they never recovered.

Sad to say, the city at the end of the first century was a mere shadow of its former glory. Worse, the church in Sardis had become like the world. Proud. Smug. Self-sufficient. Cruising on past momentum, both the city and the church were alive in name only.

If Ephesus was like New York, a bustling cosmopolitan city—if Smyrna was like Atlanta, an upcoming metropolis—if Pergamum was like Washington, D.C., the political capital—if Thyatira was like Cleveland, a blue-collar city with its labor unions—then Sardis was like Pittsburgh, where rampant unemployment has led many people into hard times.

Many churches today find themselves in just such a community. Factories closing. Middle management being laid off. Jobs moving elsewhere. It is in such an environment that the church often makes its strongest statement because God is unchanging and never in decline.

THE SPEAKER

Again, Jesus reveals Himself in a way uniquely suited for this church.

> *"And to the angel of the church in Sardis write: 'He who has the seven spirits of God, and the seven stars, says this: . . .'" (Revelation 3:1).*

HOLDING SEVEN SPIRITS

Jesus claims to be the One who possesses "the seven spirits of God." *Seven* is the number for perfection and fullness. This does not mean that there are seven Holy Spirits. There is only one Spirit of God. But when the Spirit comes, He comes in full and perfect power. Only a Spirit-energized revival can inflame hearts, energize worship, convict of sin, grant repentance, lift burdens, and empower ministry.

The key to revival in this—and any—dead church lies with Christ. Only Jesus can send the power of the Holy Spirit upon a congregation. And only the Holy Spirit can revive the church.

Revival comes only by divine prerogative. Not by man's doing. The prophet Zechariah said, "'Not by might nor by power, but by My Spirit,' says the Lord of Hosts" (Zechariah 4:6).

HOLDING SEVEN STARS

Likewise, Jesus holds "the seven stars" in His right hand. These are His pastors and spiritual leaders in the church (Revelation 1:20). Jesus will send revival to a congregation primarily through Spirit-filled pastors who minister God's Word.

Jesus holds His pastors in His right hand—a place of highest honor, strictest accountability, and greatest usability. He sovereignly places them where He can best use them.

Why these two designations together? Why is Jesus holding *both* seven spirits *and* seven stars? The key to reviving new life in a dead church lies with the Spirit's ministry in the lives of its pastor and spiritual leaders. Revival must start at the top and spread downward. Pastors must catch fire if the people are to catch fire. Like pastor, like people.

The preaching of Jonah in Nineveh sparked the greatest spontaneous movement of God recorded anywhere in Scripture. Jonah preached God's message, and over 100,000 were saved.

But the greatest obstacle was not found in the sin and corruption of Nineveh, great as that was. Nor was it found in that city's graft-ridden police force. Nor in its corrupt politicians. It was not in the false cults or pagan religions either.

The biggest obstacle to the salvation of Nineveh was found in the heart of the pious, prejudiced preacher named Jonah. Only when the prophet got right with God in the belly of the great fish was the power of the Holy Spirit released upon Nineveh.

Jonah was the key to revival in Nineveh. Likewise, pastors today are the key to revival in the church. No church can go beyond its leadership.

God's servants—pastors, elders, deacons—must be spiritually empowered men. As the leaders yield their lives to Him, God sends the Spirit's power upon them to lead them to lead the church in revival.

Pray for such men. Any church takes on the priorities, the passion, and the personality of its leaders. For good or for bad, any church will take on the heartbeat of its spiritual leadership. How important it is that a church's pastor be in tune with God.

Pray for the pastors of our country. Unquestionably, they are the keys for the power of the Holy Spirit to be unleashed in our nation.

THE SIN

With each of the four previous churches, Jesus begins with a word of commendation. But when Jesus speaks to this church, He starts with a word of criticism. Why? Jesus is so displeased with a dead church that He speaks directly to the issue. Truth is, a dead church will do more to hold back the cause of Christ than all the persecution the world can mount. A dead church threatens the very lifeblood of Christianity. Jesus hates dead religion.

So, Jesus begins this letter with a word of complaint against this church. Not a word of commendation. He begins with a stinging rebuke. A harsh criticism. He writes:

> *"I know your deeds, that you have a name that you are alive, and you are dead" (Revelation 3:1).*

Ouch! Jesus starts confrontationally because He hates dead religion. He loathes the hypocrisy of spiritual pretense. Jesus received prostitutes and drunkards with open arms. But He reserved His severest scorn for the self-righteous Pharisees.

Jesus says that they are simply cruising on past glory and have the stench of death. What does it mean, "you are dead"? It doesn't mean

that they were spiritually lost. The Bible says that those without
Christ are dead in trespasses and sins (Ephesians 2:1). But this death
in the church at Sardis means that the spiritual vitality of the members was nonexistent. They were suffering kingdom dry rot. They
had eroded into a spiritual desert. They were just going through the
empty and hollow motions of worship. They had sunk into a deep
sleep.

In the local community of Sardis, this church had built up quite
an impressive reputation. First Church Sardis was the place to be. It
was highly revered and respected. No doubt, they prided themselves
on their illustrious past.

But that was the problem. They lived in the past. In the present,
they had only an empty, lifeless profession. They had a superficial
estimate of themselves. They did not know that their spiritual lives
were dead.

Reputations are a funny thing. We care more about what we
think people think about us than what they actually think about us.

Someone has said, when we turn 20 we worry about what people think about us. When we turn 40, we stop worrying about what
others think about us. When we turn 60, we realize that no one has
been thinking about us at all.

That was the problem with the Sardis church. They so prided
their reputation built up in the past that they lost all spiritual power
in the present.

The Sardis church was outwardly active. They had all the signs
of dynamic ministry. But their inward condition was dead. They
were living off yesterday's spiritual momentum. Their vitality was
gone. A spiritual malady had paralyzed their bodies. Their spiritual
pulse was gone. They had disintegrated into spiritual barrenness. A
cold, formal rigidness had set in. A ghastly, hollow pretense
enveloped the church.

Have you ever been in a dead church like that?

Dr. Vance Havner once said that spiritual ministries go through
four stages. First, there is a man, then there is a movement, then
there is a machine, and then there is a monument. Well, this church
was at the monument stage. More correctly, the *mausoleum* stage.

What does a dead church look like?

First, there is *dead preaching*. In the pulpit, a mild-mannered man speaks to mild-mannered people, encouraging them to be more mild-mannered. His messages are filled with poems, book reviews, personal opinions, social commentary, and human interest stories. He has eloquence, but no unction. He has proper diction, but no dynamic. He is like an old heater that has broken—the blower is still working, but the heat is gone.

Second, dead churches have *dead worship*. It's like walking into a wax museum. There's no excitement. No celebration. They worship as if Jesus Christ were still dead and buried in the grave. They begin at 11:00 *sharp* and get out at 12:00 *dull*. There are no "Amens," only yawns. The congregational singing sounds like two calves dying in a hailstorm. It's so cold in those churches, you have to ice-skate down the center aisle to come forward.

Third, dead churches have *dead ministry*. There is no evangelism. No missions outreach. No church growth. Cobwebs are spun in the baptistery. Dust collect ons the church membership roll. Who would want to join this cemetery?

Oliver Cromwell was once faced with a shortage of precious metal for coins. So he sent his troops out to find some. When they returned, they reported that the only precious metal was to be found in the statues of the saints standing in the corners of churches.

Cromwell said, "Well, melt down the saints and put them in circulation."

That's the problem in dead churches. The saints are no longer in circulation and need to be melted down.

Fourth, dead churches have a *dead hope*. All they do is live in the past. At the bottom of the church stationery, they proudly display their church motto: "We've never done it that way before." They worship at the shrine of their tradition. They live in the good old days. They don't have revivals; they have reunions.

Dr. W. A. Criswell, the recently retired and noted pastor of First Baptist Church in Dallas, Texas, tells the following story. He and his wife were on vacation. The two of them were in a very remote place near a tourist haven. When Sunday came, they decided to go to church, but to not call ahead to alert the pastor. At the time, Dr. Criswell was the president of the Southern Baptist Convention.

So the Criswells slipped into the service anonymously. Dr. Criswell said that was the deadest church service he had ever attended. The preaching was dead. The ushers were mummies. The people were lifeless. At the end of the service, the pastor gave an invitation to join the church.

Dr. Criswell thought, "Who would want to join this?"

As they left church, nobody said a word to them. The Criswells got in their car and drove to a little restaurant down the way. They were not ready for what they were about to experience.

As Dr. Criswell drove up to the front door, an attendant came running out and opened Mrs. Criswell's door. He then came around and opened Dr. Criswell's door and parked their car.

They walked into the restaurant, and the *maitre d'* greeted them at the front door with a warm smile and a handshake. He was dressed nicely in a tuxedo. With a vibrant voice, he beamed, "We are so glad that you're here today. We have just the perfect table for you." He personally walked them to an attractively prepared table.

The ambience was alive. There were bright red-and-white checkered tablecloths on all the tables. Freshly cut flowers adorned the centerpiece.

Within seconds, a young college student came running out with two glasses of water. He put them on the table and said, "We're so glad that you're here. Thanks for coming. If there is anything I can get you, just let me know."

Immediately, the waiter came. He said, "I'll be your waiter today. Whatever you want or need, I'm here to serve you." When the waiter brought out the meal, it was well cooked and hot.

At the close of the meal, everyone in the kitchen came out and sang "Happy Birthday" to Mrs. Criswell. The Criswells soon felt a part of this warm family. When it came time to leave, the host walked them to the door, patted them on the back, and said, "Please come back your very first opportunity."

As they walked to their car, Dr. Criswell stopped, turned around, and looked back at this spectacle. He said to his wife, "If they would have given a public invitation to join this restaurant, I would have joined this restaurant before I would have joined that church."

I think I would have, too!

When a church is alive, it has a spiritual dynamic. You sense that God is alive and at work there. You can *feel* it!

Tragically, other churches don't know the difference between dignity and *rigor mortis*. Their worship service is more like a funeral service. Don't misunderstand me. I'm not suggesting that we get carried away in church with wild, cheerleader emotionalism. That draws attention to ourselves and distracts others. But we should have an emotional, heartfelt love for Jesus Christ that is contagious.

The church is a spiritual organism, not a lifeless organization. A spiritual entity can function only when empowered by the Holy Spirit. We don't need more resources, larger budgets, greater technology, or more sophisticated organizational charts. Ultimately, what we need is the supernatural, sovereign power of God unleashed in our churches.

We need a true revival in the power of God's Holy Spirit. One that is heaven-sent, Christ-exalting, Spirit-convicting, sin-purging, world-rejecting, and soul-saving. Only Christ can send such a revival to His church. Only He can send the Holy Spirit with supernatural power.

The kingdom of God can never be propped up with lifeless, man-made programs. Only God can raise the dead. The church is a sleeping giant that needs to be resurrected, and only the power of God can do this.

Is your spiritual life like this church? Are you dry, dormant, and dull? Are you *dead?*

Maybe you once had a close walk with the Lord, and everybody looked up to you as a dynamic Christian. But no longer. Now, you're *dead*.

Maybe you once taught a Bible study and were known for your ministry. But now, your ministry is *dead*.

Maybe you once were a dynamic witness for Christ. God used to use you to lead people to Christ regularly. But now nobody is being won to Christ. Your personal evangelism is *dead*.

You once read your Bible every day. But now, your personal devotions are *dead*.

Could this be you?

THE SOLUTION

How can you experience revival? How can you be raised from the dead? Jesus gives us five key commands that lead to revival. He writes:

*"Wake up, and strengthen the things that remain, which were about to die;
for I have not found your deeds completed in the sight of My God.
Remember therefore what you have received and heard; and keep it, and
repent. If therefore you will not wake up, I will come like a thief, and you
will not know at what hour I will come upon you" (Revelation 3:2-3).*

STEP ONE: WAKE UP!

First, *wake up!* Jesus says to this church of zombies, "Wake up!"
When we are spiritually dead, we need a slap in the face to awaken
us. A splash of cold water. A sniff of ammonia. We need God's alarm
to go off.

Jesus is saying, "Come out of your spiritual hibernation! Arouse
yourself."

There must be an awareness that something is wrong. Honestly
face your dullness. Admit the dryness of your spiritual life. Catch a
whiff of the reeking corruption of your death. Admit to God that
something is missing.

Admit it. You need a spiritual awakening!

When I first came to the church which I now pastor, I used to
close the morning worship service by calling on someone in the congregation to pray.

One particular Sunday, I preached my heart out and concluded
by calling on a man—one of our deacons—to close the service with
prayer. Unfortunately, I did not realize that he had gone to sleep during my sermon.

When I called his name over the loudspeaker, he instantly jerked
his head back and groaned out loud. The entire congregation could
hear his gasp. He sounded like a whale surfacing for air. Needless to
say, I've been more careful whom I call on publicly.

Those who are asleep in church need to wake up before they are
called out by God.

STEP TWO: FORGE AHEAD!

Second, *forge ahead!* Jesus says that they must "strengthen the things
that remain, which were about to die." It's not enough just to wake
up. This refers to the basics of the spiritual life—Bible study, prayer,

worship, and fellowship. Jesus is saying, "Get back into the Word! Get back into prayer! Get back into fellowship! Get back to the basics!"

We must throw off the covers. And get out of bed. We must get dressed and get with it.

Maybe you need to start a Bible reading plan. Or perhaps you need to set aside a regular time each day to pray. Perhaps you need to get back to attending church regularly. Whatever. But strengthen what remains.

STEP THREE: LOOK BACK!

Third, *look back!* Jesus says, "Remember therefore what you have received and heard." What had they received and heard at the beginning?

The gospel. They had received the basic truths of the Christian life. This is not a call to live in the past, but a command to remember their rich spiritual heritage in Christ.

Jesus is saying here, "*Remember* how you were saved! *Remember* how you were nothing before God found you. *Remember* how God's grace reached down and redeemed you!"

STEP FOUR: HOLD ON!

Fourth, *hold on!* Jesus goes on to say, "and keep it." Here is Christ's appeal to obey God's Word—to keep His commandments—in every area of their lives. Disobedience and spiritual dryness are twin sisters. Wherever you find one, you will be sure to find the other.

Jesus is saying, "Weave God's truth through every area of your life. Keep the Word! Put it into practice." Where God has put a period, don't put a question mark. Selective obedience is no obedience at all. It's merely convenience. Get back to obeying God's Word.

A husband and wife were discussing the possibility of taking a trip to the Holy Land.

"Wouldn't it be fantastic to go to the Holy Land," he said, "and stand and shout the Ten Commandments from Mount Sinai?"

"It would be better," his wife pointedly said, "if we stayed home and kept them."

STEP FIVE: LET GO!

Fifth, *let go!* Jesus says, finally, "Repent." This calls for an immediate decision to turn around and come back to Christ with all one's heart. Repentance calls for a quick and decisive change of thought, devotion, and behavior.

In calling for repentance, Jesus is saying, "Confess your sin of spiritual lethargy. Turn away from it. Do an immediate aboutface! Return to full devotion to Christ. Change your life!"

Repentance means to let go of our sins. That's a choice that each of us must make.

A little boy once got his hand caught inside his mother's expensive vase. She was most upset!

She applied soapsuds to his hand. Then cooking oil. Even shampoo. But nothing would work. Finally, she got a hammer and was ready to sacrifice the priceless vase in order to rescue her son's swollen hand.

As she pulled the hammer back, ready to smash the family heirloom, the frightened boy cried out, "Would it help if I let go of all the pennies?"

All too often, that's our problem. We don't want to let go of the world. We risk the truly valuable because we will not let go of our sin. We must turn loose of sin if we are to turn our lives around.

STEP SIX: LOOK OUT!

What if they don't repent? Jesus warns that He will come like a thief to any church that will not wake up and get with it!

This is not a reference to the second coming of Christ. Rather, it points to a sudden coming of Christ to judge this church. To remove their lampstand. To discipline them.

If they do not repent, Jesus will come like a thief. Unexpectedly. Unannounced. To steal what is valuable—whatever ministry opportunity remains.

Why would Jesus threaten to deal so harshly with this church? Because nothing holds back the spread of the gospel like a dead, lifeless church. Persecution causes the church to grow. But spiritual deadness is like a malignant cancer that spreads to the whole body. It renders the church impotent, ineffective, and inactive.

I heard about a pastor who noticed that one of his parishioners had not been at church in several months. So he decided to make a personal call.

The pastor went by the man's house. He said, "We sure have been missing you in church."

"Well," the man said, fishing for any excuse, "it's been raining the past few Sundays, and I didn't want to get wet."

"I know, but it's been dry in church," retorted the pastor.

"Yeah, and that's *another* reason," the parishioner wryly replied.

A dry church will do more to harm the cause of Christ than almost anything else. It is a sin to bore people with the gospel of Jesus Christ.

THE STRENGTH

At last, Jesus commends this church. He finally has something good to say about this congregation. Every good tree does bear good fruit.

There is a faithful remnant here. A committed core group remains. It is to these diehards that Jesus speaks encouragement.

> *"But you have a few people in Sardis who have not soiled their garments; and they will walk with Me in white; for they are worthy" (Revelation 3:4).*

There were a few people in Sardis who were still spiritually vibrant. Some were still alive and awake in their faith. This core group had abstained from moral impurity. They had not compromised with the world around them. They had not grown comfortable with the godless culture.

They were walking in white garments, picturing their moral purity. They refused to soil their robes with the world's filth. Because they had not yielded to temptation, Jesus promises to replace their human garments with specially prepared white robes. The anticipation of wearing such holy apparel should strongly motivate them to remain pure today.

In which group do you find yourself? Are you in the larger group that is spiritually dead? Or a part of the committed core? Are you a part of your church's problem? Or a part of the solution? Are you a pillar in your church? Or a caterpillar that just crawls in and out?

This remnant has remained true to God. While escaping the world's pollution, they have lived holy and righteous lives. They have not loved the world, nor the things in the world. While the vast majority in the church have been lulled to sleep, this group has remained spiritually awake and alert.

THE SUCCESS

You may have heard it said that some people are so heavenly-minded that they are no earthly good. Actually, just the opposite is usually the case. Most of us are not heavenly-minded enough. So, Jesus concludes by reminding this church of the reward that awaits them in heaven.

Christ recognized the connection between our heavenly reward and our present motivation. The former inspires the latter. The hope of future glory awakens present holiness.

Here's what awaits those who follow Him:

> *"He who overcomes shall thus be clothed in white garments; and I will not erase his name from the book of life, and I will confess his name before My Father, and before His angels" (Revelation 3:5).*

To all who overcome spiritual deadness, Jesus makes three promises: white garments, a permanent record, and a heavenly confession.

WHITE GARMENTS

First, *white garments.* Jesus promises, "He who overcomes shall thus be clothed in white garments." These garments, a brilliant white, picture our eternal state of righteousness in heaven. We will be fully cleansed and made spotless by the blood of Christ. Like laundered, dirty garments, every vestige of sin will be taken off; and like new, clean garments, a perfect righteousness will be put on. This would have been especially meaningful to people who lived where woolen garments were manufactured. Here is a promise of eternal righteousness.

ETERNAL SECURITY

Second, *a permanent record.* Jesus says, "And I will not erase his name from the book of life." Does this mean that it is possible to have your name blotted out of the book of life? Does this mean that a Christian can lose his or her salvation?

Unquestionably, the Bible teaches the eternal security of the believer. Once saved, always saved. So, what is Jesus promising here?

An understanding of the historical background is helpful here. In John's day, a king kept an official register that contained all the names of its citizens. A name would be removed if one committed a crime against the state. Or a name would be blotted out if a citizen moved, or if he died. The book contained the names of all true citizens who had not rebelled against him.

Conversely, Jesus will never blot our names out of His book. This is not a threat, indicating that a believer can lose his or her salvation. Actually, He is saying the very opposite. Regardless of what sin a believer will ever commit—even the sin of spiritual apathy or deadness—Christ will never blot his name out of His book of life. This is a positive promise stated by a double negative ("not erase").

Actually, the names of God's elect were written in the book of life from the foundation of the world (Revelation 13:8; 17:8). Before we were even born, the names of all believers were written in God's book—before they had done anything good or bad. We were chosen in Christ before the beginning of time. What is predestined before time is settled for all time.

DIVINE CONFESSION

Third, *a heavenly confession*. Jesus promises, "And I will confess his name before My Father, and before His angels." As our Advocate with the Father, Jesus promises that He will acknowledge every name in the book of life. At the final judgment, Christ will confess all true believers before God in heaven. This courtroom scene, in the presence of holy angels, will vindicate the salvation of all God's redeemed. However, all unbelievers will be excluded from heaven.

Apparently, many in Sardis were ashamed to publicly confess Christ. In the pressure of a godless culture, they were failing in this way. To such faltering disciples, Jesus said, "Everyone therefore who shall confess Me before men, I will also confess him before My Father who is in heaven. But whoever shall deny Me before men, I will also deny him before My Father who is in heaven" (Matthew 10:32-33).

THE SUMMONS

Finally, Jesus concludes with a call to hear. Here is the familiar invitation:

> *"He who has an ear, let him hear what the Spirit says to the churches"*
> *(Revelation 3:6).*

Here is Jesus' individual call, inviting each hearer to respond. The Holy Spirit has spoken through Jesus' words to the churches; but truth must be acted upon. The plural ("churches") reminds us that this message is intended for every church in every generation. Each church and every believer will profit greatly from this letter.

In summary, what is the Spirit saying here? This letter has addressed the danger of *spiritual deadness*. Sardis had a reputation of being vibrant, but, in reality, she was dead. Her devotion to Christ was stagnant.

What this church lacked, Christ offered to give—a new vitality and restored passion for God. But these believers must do their part. They must *wake up* to their dead condition, *forge ahead* in pursuing God, *look back* to earlier days of spiritual passion, *hold* on to Christ's commandments, *let go* of sin—*let go* of sin or *look out* for Christ's discipline.

The Spirit is saying, "Don't stay dead. Wake up and crawl out of the grave of apathy and complacency."

A man once came to Gypsy Smith, the celebrated English evangelist of an earlier time, and asked him how to have revival.

Gypsy asked, "Do you have a place where you can pray?"

"Yes," was the reply.

"I'll tell you what you must do," said the evangelist. "You go to that place and take a piece of chalk along. Kneel down there and with the chalk draw a complete circle all around you.

"Then pray for God to send revival on everyone inside of the circle. Stay there until He answers—and you will have revival."

Perhaps that's what you need to do. Get alone with God and ask Him to send revival to your heart. Don't get up until He has. Stay there until He answers.

And you *will* have revival.

IX

LITTLE CHURCH
WITH A BIG GOD

Revelation 3:7–13

CERTAIN MEN SEEM TO RISE ABOVE the landscape of their day and mark out their generation for Jesus Christ. Donald Grey Barnhouse was one of those spiritual giants.

As the pastor of the Tenth Presbyterian Church of downtown Philadelphia, Pennsylvania, Dr. Barnhouse towered above his times and left his impact for eternity. Soon after graduating from Princeton Theological Seminary, Barnhouse was invited back to campus to preach in chapel.

For a young pastor, this was quite an intimidating experience. As Barnhouse stepped into the pulpit to address the student body and faculty, he was suddenly quite nervous.

In attendance that day was one of the most brilliant men on the face of the earth —an Old Testament professor named Dr. Robert Dick Wilson. Professor Wilson was a genius who reportedly spoke twenty-seven languages and was highly respected worldwide for his proven scholarship in the Scriptures.

As Barnhouse stood to speak, Dr. Wilson sat with arms folded on the front row of the chapel, peering stoically over the top of his glasses. The young pastor preached the best he could, but he found it difficult not to be preoccupied with his famous professor seated so prominently at his feet.

"What is Dr. Wilson thinking?" Barnhouse wondered. "Does he approve?"

Then, suddenly, a disturbing thing occurred!

Midway through Barnhouse's chapel message, Professor Wilson shuffled his papers together. He stood to his feet and *walked out of the chapel* . . . while Barnhouse was still speaking.

Barnhouse was crushed!

What had he said to offend Dr. Wilson? Where had he failed? Was his theology wrong? Was his use of the original languages improper? Barnhouse could barely gather the strength to finish his message.

After the chapel ordeal was over, the young preacher exchanged a few polite pleasantries with well-wishers and then went straight to the revered professor's office. He knocked on the door and, with a trembling voice, asked, "Where did I fail?"

Dr. Wilson stopped his reading and looked up. "Fail? Oh, you didn't fail," Wilson explained. "I always come to hear my former students speak one time. I simply want to know if they are a *big-Godder* or a *small-Godder*. I am very pleased that you are one of our few graduates who is a *big-Godder*. You preach a big God. I didn't need to hear any more."

What a lesson for Barnhouse!

What a lesson for *us*!

Those who believe in a great God are those who do great things for God. He delights in taking ordinary people and doing extraordinary things through them. That way, the greatness belongs to Him.

There is one holy passion that beats in the heart of every Spirit-filled believer. It is an ambition to know God and to do something great for Him. Whether it be a pastor toward his ministry, a businessman toward his career, or a parent toward his or her child, every Christian wants his or her life to count for eternity. The key for making one's life strategically count for Jesus Christ is to be gripped with a high view of God.

Are you a *big-Godder*?

Do you serve a great and awesome God?

These are life-determining questions. In fact, these are the most important questions that we can ask ourselves. Answer them correctly, and great will be our influence for the kingdom of God.

The size of our God will determine the impact of our lives. Churches with a big God conduct extraordinary ministry. *Big-Godders* shake this world for Christ.

That's what makes our Lord's next letter so important. It is addressed to the church at Philadelphia. They ministered in one of the smallest of the seven cities, and yet the believers there had the greatest opportunity for ministry before them. Why? Because they had the biggest God.

The same is true for any individual, ministry, or church today. Ordinary people do extraordinary things when their eyes are upon a great God. Let's learn how faith in a big God works.

THE SETTING

Philadelphia was a smaller city, compared to Ephesus and Smyrna. Smaller in prosperity. Smaller in productivity. Smaller in prestige. But despite its smallness, this city was strategically positioned for major impact. There are three important considerations in real estate: location, location, location. Philadelphia had all three.

Because of its location, the city of Philadelphia was a major hub of communication, disseminating information throughout this part of the known world. Strategically located. Small in stature. But significant in influence. That was Philadelphia.

Ancient travelers would pass through Philadelphia on their way to important destinations. As the "Gateway to the East," it was ideally situated to touch the lives of many people. Beyond this small settlement lay the kingdoms of Lydia, Missia, and Phrygia. Consequently, Philadelphia lay at the intersection of major highways. The armies of Caesar were known to march through Philadelphia as they went to and from Rome. Merchants would pass through Philadelphia going to and from market.

Located about 25 miles southeast of Sardis, the city was built upon an elevated hill that could be easily defended. However, it also sat on a geological fault that made the city vulnerable to volcanoes and earthquakes.

In A.D. 17 the world's most devastating earthquake rocked Philadelphia and eleven other cities, leveling the city and leaving it in shambles. In the following years, the town continued to be jolted by aftershocks. So much so that many of the residents moved out permanently to live in the surrounding fields for fear of being buried alive.

If Ephesus was like New York City—if Smyrna was like Atlanta—if Pergamum was like Washington, D. C.—if Thyatira was like Cleveland—if Sardis was like Pittsburgh—then Philadelphia was like Little Rock, Arkansas. Small in size, but strategically located. Situated on the main highway. The gateway to the vast region beyond.

THE SPEAKER

The Divine Correspondent now identifies Himself in the way He wants those in Philadelphia to see Him. Jesus wants them to know Him as holy, true, and sovereign. So, He writes:

> *"And to the angel of the church in Philadelphia write: 'He who is holy, who is true, who has the key of David, who opens and no one will shut, and who shuts and no one opens, says this: . . .'"* (Revelation 3:7).

In this self-description, Jesus does something unique. This is the only church to whom Jesus identifies Himself in a way not previously revealed in John's vision of Revelation chapter 1. This is because the vision of Christ was predominantly a vision of judgment. But as Jesus speaks to this church, He has *no* complaint or criticism. Only commendation. So, an encouraging picture of Christ is revealed here instead.

HOLY

First, Jesus reveals Himself as He who is holy. The concept of holiness comes from a Semitic root meaning "to cut." To be holy is to be a cut above. Separate. Set apart. This has two aspects.

One, His essential holiness by which He is set apart from His creation. He is majestic, transcendent, and exalted. Two, His ethical holiness by which He is set apart from all sin. He is perfectly pure and undefiled in all His ways—without moral blemish or stain.

Everything about Jesus is holy. The Head of the church is *holy* in

His character. *Holy* in His words. *Holy* in His actions. *Holy* in His purposes. He is *wholly holy*.

Jesus' holiness means that He is exclusively set apart to God. He is transcendent, lifted up above heaven and earth. Exalted upon His throne. Majestic in His glory. Radiant in His splendor. Nothing can be compared to Him. He is the incomparable Christ.

TRUE

Second, Jesus is *true*—"He . . . who is true." This self-description emphasizes not His truthfulness, but the fact that He is true. That means He is authentic or genuine. He is "the real thing"!

Jesus is no cheap imitation. No counterfeit Christ. No mimic Messiah. He is the real God who is true to His Word. He can be completely trusted because He is genuine Deity. He is not an imitation idol, but the authentic Almighty of heaven and earth.

SOVEREIGN

Third, Jesus is *sovereign*. He claims to be the One "who has the key of David, who opens and no one will shut, and who shuts and no one opens." That means He is the keeper of the keys who alone opens and shuts the door leading to God's blessings.

The Scripture referred to here is Isaiah 22:22. King Hezekiah was king over the Davidic Kingdom and was served by a man named Eliakim as the royal treasurer. Eliakim was the guardian of the king's treasures. He alone possessed the keys needed to open the royal treasure vault. Figuratively, these keys were placed "on his shoulder," signifying that he controlled all access to the king's vast treasures.

Only Eliakim could open the vault door giving access to Hezekiah's riches. But when Eliakim closed the door of the treasury, no one could open it.

Similarly, Jesus has been handed the keys of heaven's treasury by God the Father. These keys open the doors leading into the rich blessing of God's grace. Jesus is the sole guardian of the riches of God. With infinite wisdom, He controls access to His Father's spiritual riches as He deems best.

In this self-description, Jesus is claiming unrivaled sovereignty over the church. He is claiming to be the One who opens and closes the doors of salvation, circumstances, and ministry opportunities. Jesus alone unlocks access into the vast riches of God's abounding grace.

Why would Jesus reveal Himself *this* way to *this* church?

Because they had very little strength and few resources. We must be reminded that any church's strength lies not in its size, but in its God.

We live in the day of the megachurch. Large, towering churches dominate the landscape. For those who worship and serve in smaller congregations, that can be discouraging. Even intimidating. We must remember that spiritual success is not dictated by the size of the church's buildings, budgets, and buses. Rather, it is determined by having great faith in a big God.

What matters is not how big or small the church is. What truly matters is how big their God is. It is far better to be a little church with a big God than to be a big church with a little God. Little churches accomplish great ministry when they serve a holy, true, and sovereign God—a big God who can open big doors.

Successful ministry depends upon trusting Him who alone can open the door of ministry. What are you trusting God for?

THE STRENGTHS

Much could be said to commend this little church. In so many ways, this was a great church! In fact, Jesus had nothing about which to rebuke this congregation. As He walked around their lampstand, He had only praise for these believers. Here's what He writes:

> *"I know your deeds. Behold, I have put before you an open door which no one can shut, because you have a little power, and have kept My word, and have not denied My name" (Revelation 3:8).*

Of course He knows their deeds! Jesus is a firsthand, intimate observer of this church's business. He peers into every meeting; He looks into every heart; He knows all about them. Not even this small flock escapes His notice.

For this little church, Christ opens a large door. When a church faithfully meets certain spiritual conditions, Christ opens doors for them for expanded ministry opportunities.

What opens doors? Simple faithfulness to God's will. No more, no less. Faithfulness turns the key that unlocks an unlimited tomorrow. At the heart of faithfulness is faith in a sovereign God. The church at Philadelphia had it.

LITTLE POWER

First, Jesus notes that they "have a little power." This may sound like a rebuke, but it's not. It's merely a statement of fact. Compared to the other churches, they have only a little power, limited resources, small size, and little clout.

This is not a high-powered church. This is no well-oiled, high-profile, hotly-wired megachurch. They have no respected community leaders on their church boards. Nor any successful businessmen to underwrite their budget. They live from hand to mouth—God's hand to their mouth.

It was in their weakness that they learned a secret: faithfulness to God opens great doors. Even for the smallest churches.

OBEDIENCE

Second, Jesus commends them because they "kept My word." They were fiercely committed to God's Word. They preached it, taught it, believed it, obeyed it, lived it, and shared it. They wouldn't budge from the Word. Whatever they did, it was all directed and empowered by God's Word.

We need more churches like this today. Too many have fallen victim to the latest gimmicks of some church growth guru. Too many jump on the latest bandwagon for building a better, bigger church, little realizing that this parade leads nowhere. What we need, instead, is a return to keeping God's Word. Just keep the Word, and any church will be led into the abundance of God's riches.

BOLDNESS

Likewise, Jesus said they "have not denied My name." They were unashamed of the gospel. Apparently many in Philadelphia, especially unbelieving Jews, had forced some believers to disregard Christ's teaching and deny the faith.

But this little band of believers would not buckle under worldly pressure. They remained true to the Lord who redeemed them. Wherever they went in town, whether into the marketplace, their neighborhoods, or among friends, the name of Jesus was always on their lips. Boldly, they witnessed for Him in every opportunity.

No wonder Christ opened doors for this church. They were faithful in little. So God gave them opportunity to be faithful in much.

Sometimes people reason, "If God would only make me a successful businessman, then I'd give the church a lot of money." But the real issue is, "What are you doing with the money you have now?" Our faithfulness with the little God gives us determines how we will handle greater opportunities.

Here lies the secret of this church. Faithfulness. They were faithful to God with what little they had. Therefore, Christ opened before them a door leading to greater ministry opportunities. It was to this little church that Jesus said, "I have put before you an open door." No matter how small a church is, faith in a great God opens big doors.

An "open door" is a God-given opportunity for expanded ministry. Open doors lead to unlimited ministry potential for Christ. They are pivotal passages leading to golden opportunities. Open doors lead to vast new horizons.

When God opens a door, He suddenly removes all obstacles and reorders our circumstances. A new path is opened up that leads into a bright new tomorrow. It is a time when God ushers in a new day of ministry. A new era of strategic impact is brought onto the scene.

Paul was aware of open doors divinely placed before him. The apostle writes, "A wide door for effectual service has opened to me" (1 Corinthians 16:9). Later he wrote, "Now when I came to Troas for the gospel of Christ . . . a door was opened for me in the Lord" (2 Corinthians 2:12). He requested prayer "that God may open up to us a door for the word, so that we may speak forth the mystery of Christ" (Colossians 4:3).

When Paul returned to the church at Antioch, he shared all that God had done on his first missionary journey. Luke records, "And when they had arrived and gathered the church together, they began to report all things that God had done with them and how He had opened a door of faith to the Gentiles" (Acts 14:27). Paul related all their successes back to God's open door.

What open door has God placed before you? Sometimes we are blind and fail to see the open doors. Sometimes we are looking for ways to serve God when He has already opened a door right smack-dab before us. What strategic opportunity has God opened for you?

Maybe God has opened the opportunity for you to teach a Bible study class. Maybe He has opened a door for you to reach out to your next-door neighbor. Maybe He has opened a door for you to use a special talent or spiritual gift in your church. Do you see the open door that God has put before you?

GOD'S OPEN DOOR POLICY

Here are some key principles—"God's Open Door Policy"—that reveal how God works through open doors. Here are timeless truths regarding doors that only God can open.

1. *God sovereignly opens doors for His people.* Only Christ can open doors leading into His will. He alone has the keys. When our circumstances seem to be most impossible, that is when God most delights to open doors for His people. This demands that we pray to Him who alone can open the door to effective ministry.

Witness Moses leading the children of God out of Egypt to the Promised Land. Pharaoh and his hordes were in hot pursuit. Unexpectedly, the people of God found themselves trapped between a rock and a hard place. So Moses raised his rod to God. And God opened a door for them—a door leading right through the Red Sea!

What door are you asking Him to open? A door to witness to someone? A door to serve those who are in need?

2. *God's open doors are only seen with the eyes of faith.* Natural eyes see only the impossibilities. Physical eyes see only the obstacles. Only spiritual eyes can see God's doors opening before us. Only faith can see God-given opportunities. "Now faith is the assurance of things hoped for, the conviction of things not seen" (Hebrews 11:1).

3. *An open door requires our step of faith.* It's not enough just to see and admire an open door. We must take a step of faith and move forward. God's part is to open the door, but our part is to go through it.

What door has God opened for you? Step out by faith and enter it.

4. *Unbelief sees the obstacles, but faith sees the opportunities.* An open door always implies that there is also a massive wall. Unbelief looks at the barriers, obstacles, and difficulties, while faith is focused upon the open door. Unbelief says, "The obstacles are too great. It costs too much. It'll never work. People will never buy it. We've never done it that way before." But faith says, "Here's an open door. Let's go through it!"

Caleb and Joshua saw the opportunity, not the obstacles. The other ten spies could only see the giants in the land. But Caleb and Joshua saw what a giant their God was.

The Chinese word for *crisis* is a combination of symbols for "danger" plus "opportunity." That's the way it is in God's kingdom. Opportunity usually comes in the face of crisis and danger.

5. *Doors now open are quickly closing.* When God opens an opportunity, it will not stay open forever. There is a day—an appointed time, a divinely designated season—for that door to be open. But it will eventually be closed. Perhaps soon.

It's like harvesttime. The farmer has worked hard preparing the soil, planting the seed, and growing the crop. When harvesttime comes, the crop must be captured today. Harvesttime is no time to be painting the barn. No time to be oiling the tractor. No time to be planting flowers around the house. All that must be left for another day. The harvest must be gathered now or never.

So it is in God's kingdom. When He opens a door before us, we must act promptly. If not, the door will soon be closed.

6. *A church must go through an open door together.* As God opened this door for the church, it required harmony, unity, and togetherness. Only as they acted together could they capture the opportunity at hand. They must go forward by faith as one body—undivided!

When I was in high school, I played football. After we had warmed up before the game, we would return to the locker room for final instructions. Then we would come back onto the field together. We would gather together behind the goalposts, and the cheerleaders would put up a big pep banner across the goalposts. The band would play our school fight song, and we would run through the pep banner together.

That's the way God wants the church to be. United. Running through the door of opportunity together into the future.

7. *If God is with us, nothing can stop us.* Jesus says, "I have put before you an open door which no one can shut." If God opened it, only God can close it. Satan can't close it. Demons can't. Imposing circumstances can't. A hostile government can't. An unbelieving world can't. Nobody can close it. God opened it, and only God can close it.

This world is not friendly to the church of Christ. The spiritual warfare is heating up as never before. But we must be assured that as long as God desires a door of ministry opportunity to remain open, it will. Nothing and no one can close it.

THE SUFFERING

Whenever God opens the door of heaven to bless us, Satan will open the gates of hell to blast us. Whenever a church moves forward by faith, it is sure to meet the Devil head-on. That's precisely what happened in Philadelphia. Jesus notes:

> *"Behold, I will cause those of the synagogue of Satan, who say that they are Jews, and are not, but lie—behold, I will make them to come and bow down at your feet, and to know that I have loved you. Because you have kept the word of My perseverance, I also will keep you from the hour of testing, that hour which is about to come upon the whole world, to test those who dwell upon the earth" (Revelation 3:9-10).*

Their suffering came in the name of religion. In Philadelphia, there was a group of Jews who met locally in a synagogue. They claimed to be true sons of Father Abraham, but they weren't. They professed faith in God, but they lied. They were unbelieving Jews, and Satan was their father. Whenever they met to worship, Jesus said, they were the "synagogue of Satan."

These Jews were persecuting the church, slandering them and spreading vicious lies. The opposition was widespread and resulted in great harm for the believers.

Jesus personally knew all about this. He Himself had been the target of Satan's synagogue during the days of His earthly ministry. It was the religious Pharisees who leveled the greatest hatred against

Jesus. Despite their claims to be true sons of Abraham, Jesus told them, "You are of your father the Devil" (John 8:44). He says here, "You attend the synagogue of Satan." Same message, different group.

Religion without regeneration is a cruel thing. It was a religious crowd that crucified Jesus. Religious zeal without the saving knowledge of God is the worst form of human depravity.

Despite this attack upon the church, Jesus promises to make these unbelievers bow down before them and acknowledge their true relationship with God. How could such a dramatic change occur? How could their hearts be changed this radically?

The gospel. The saving gospel that Jesus is the dynamite of God unto those who believe. To all who repent and believe, Jesus promises to convert His enemies and bring them to their knees. The gospel can save the greatest sinners and transform them into humble saints.

That is precisely what happened. Rather than back down, the church kept on preaching Christ and witnessing to the community. And God used their faithful testimony to convert these unbelieving Jews. In dramatic fashion, the Lord used the simple preaching of His Word to save sinners.

That's what is needed today. A restored confidence in preaching the gospel to convert the lost. Certainly the enemies of the church are great today. But the power of the gospel is far greater. The grace of God is able to capture lost sinners, bound in the golden chains of the gospel, and to bring them to kneel at Jesus' feet.

Jesus promises to keep this church secure from "the hour of testing." With sober reality, Jesus points out that their city will become even more ungodly. Their world would become even more hostile to Christianity. But Jesus promises to keep them through these coming perilous times.

The "hour of testing" was coming their way. Roman persecution would soon be coming to this city. In the face of such tribulation, Jesus promises to protect them from the gathering storm.

This promise of deliverance was not made to other churches. Some would go through the flames. Jesus actually promised the church in Smyrna that they would suffer future persecution. But for this Philadelphian church, Jesus said, "I will keep you from the hour of testing."

Amazingly, some churches meet with prosperity, while others

experience persecution. This is all according to God's sovereign will. Philadelphia is promised deliverance, and yet Smyrna is promised persecution. Mysterious and strange is God's sovereign will.

We have seen such divine discrimination in our own day. While the church in America has experienced great prosperity for 300 years, the church in China, Russia, and Africa has experienced persecution. All this is according to God's sovereign plan.

THE SUCCESS

Jesus concludes with His usual word of hope and comfort. He promises blessing to every overcomer in Christ. The overcomer is the one who holds fast to Christ's Word in the face of mounting adversity and opposition. To these overcomers, Jesus writes:

> *"He who overcomes, I will make him a pillar in the temple of My God, and he will not go out from it any more; and I will write upon him the name of My God . . . and My new name" (Revelation 3:12).*

This is a staggering promise! Here is His guarantee of our eternal security, absolute assurance, and a deeper knowledge of Himself.

A PILLAR IN GOD'S TEMPLE

First, Jesus promises, "I will make him a pillar in the temple of My God." A pillar is an ancient symbol of security and strength. When all else has fallen, a pillar remains strong and erect.

In ancient times, a distinguished citizen would have a pillar erected in his honor. He might be a noted senator, a noble dignitary, a famous philosopher, or a respected educator. His name would be inscribed upon a massive pillar to document his contribution for future generations to see.

Drawing upon this ancient practice, Jesus said that overcomers will receive such recognition in heaven. All faithful service for Christ will never be forgotten. Better than having our name written upon one of the pillars, we will *be* pillars in the temple of God. Now, that's eternal security.

In addition, Jesus says, "he will not go out from it any more." Remember, Philadelphia sat on a fault line near the epicenter of the massive earthquake of A.D. 17. Buildings, debris, and rubble came tumbling down upon the citizens as they ran out of town for safety. Aftershocks served as reminders of threatening danger.

Many were too terrified to move back. Others who did return lived in constant fear of another earthquake. So the slightest tremor sent the citizens of Philadelphia scurrying out of town.

By contrast, Jesus says we will never leave the presence of God. He will make us a permanent fixture in the heavenly temple.

THREE NEW NAMES

Jesus also promises, "And I will write upon him the name of My God." In that day, writing your name upon something was a mark of ownership. A master would write his name upon his servants. Like a brand on cattle, the master's name meant that the servant belonged to him.

To receive God's name is equivalent to belonging to God. That relationship can never be broken. His name is inscribed permanently upon His servants. We are His forever!

Moreover, Jesus says that "I will write upon him . . . the name of the city of My God, the new Jerusalem, which comes down out of heaven from My God." Overcomers will receive all the rights of citizenship in the new Jerusalem.

This heavenly citizenship will mean the removal of all pain and sorrow, access to the water of life, eating from the tree of life, serving Christ, seeing His face, reigning with Him, and deliverance from all ungodly people (Revelation 21—22).

Finally, Jesus promises, "I will write upon him . . . My new name." Even better than having the name of the new Jerusalem written upon us is having Jesus' name.

Christ's name symbolizes the full revelation of His divine person. Presently, we can't even begin to grasp the full magnitude of His unveiled glory. But at the time of our arrival into heaven, we shall know Him—exponentially so.

A person's name represents his character. For example, a good name signifies a good reputation and character. In Christ's glory at God's right hand, God has given Him a new name representing the unveiling of His divine majesty.

One day we, as overcomers, will see Christ face to face and will behold His glory. Overwhelmed in amazement, we will grow beyond all present thoughts in our knowledge of Him.

THE SUMMONS

Like precious seed, the truths of this letter must fall upon fertile soil prepared by the Holy Spirit. If we do not heed this message, then Christ's words are of no avail. So, Jesus writes:

> *"He who has an ear, let him hear what the Spirit says to the churches"*
> *(Revelation 3:13).*

Again, we are reminded to pay special attention to Christ's words. Jesus is the speaker, and the Spirit is calling out to every church and every Christian. This message is critically important. To hear and not to obey is not to hear at all.

What is the Spirit saying?

Our faithfulness in small matters opens up greater ministry opportunities in the future. No church is limited by its size. We are only limited by the size of our God. Faith in a great God opens up great doors for ministry. No matter how small the church. God often does His greatest work through His weakest and most obscure instruments.

Are you a *big-Godder*? How big is your God? Do you have faith in a big God? Or is your God too small?

If we have faith in a big God, even the smallest task is important.

A construction foreman once approached one of his workers who was busy laying bricks at the foundation of a new church. The foreman asked, "What are you doing?"

The laborer said, "Can't you see? I'm laying bricks."

The foreman then proceeded to another bricklayer and asked, "What are you doing?"

The second laborer said, "I'm building a church."

The foreman then walked over to a third bricklayer and asked the same question—"What are you doing?"

But this man had a totally different perspective. He answered, "I'm building a house of worship for the glory of God."

All three were doing the same work. But the first two were occupied only with the task. Only the third man saw the big picture. He lived to serve a great God.

How about you? Are you just laying bricks? Or do you live to serve a great God?

Let me ask you one more time: are you a *big-Godder*?

X

IT MAKES GOD SICK!

Revelation 3:14–22

PULSATING PAIN HITS ME like an oncoming freight train, reminding me it's Monday morning. With every beat of my heart, icepick-like pain is driven deeper into my skull. It is excruciating. Agonizing. Torturing.

It always occurs on Monday. Never on Tuesday. Never on Friday. Always on *Monday*.

Monday morning is when these massive migraines always strike me and leave me paralyzed and immobilized for the next twelve hours. What a day off!

These headaches make me want to screw my head off. Anything to relieve the pain. My temples are throbbing as though in a vise grip that is ever tightening. The torturous pain centers in an eye socket, a forehead, or my neck.

But that's not the worst part.

The most debilitating part is the onslaught of nausea. My impaled stomach becomes so upset, it feels like an angry volcano ready to erupt.

When I wake up with the headache, I try to hold it off with pain relievers. But I eventually succumb to its agonizing grip, which overpowers me. Squirming in bed, I try to sleep it off. But who can sleep with such pain? I will eventually throw up and become so weak that I collapse asleep from sheer exhaustion.

In a few hours, I'll wake up and come to my senses. Only to throw up again. Then I'll collapse back into sleep until late in the afternoon, reduced to mere vegetable status. Whew! What makes me so ill? What makes me so sick? Why does it always strike on Monday morning?

There's no mystery about what causes this sickness. Monday *always* follows Sunday. And Sunday means church. What inflicts this pain upon me is *church*.

As a pastor, church on Sunday absolutely wipes me out. Physically. Emotionally. Spiritually. Leaving home at 5:45 A.M. and not returning until 9:30 P.M. leaves me drained. Preaching three times. Praying. Counseling. Visiting. Committee meetings. Greeting visitors. Making announcements. Listening to complaints. Finding lost items. Fixing the copy machine. Rewriting my sermon notes. Kissing babies. Meeting relatives. Staying until the last person leaves. Not eating until 10:00 P.M.

Church. I spend a month at church every Sunday. It often takes more out of me than I have to give. It can literally make me sick!

Would you believe that church can make our Lord *sick* as well? Do you know that it often leaves Him *nauseated*? Church can make Christ *ill* to His stomach. It can make Him want to *throw up*.

What about church would make Jesus so sick to His stomach? What about His people could possibly cause Him such a violent reaction?

Lukewarmness.

Spiritual indifference in the church makes Christ want to throw up. Apathy makes our Lord ill. Lukewarm preaching. Indifferent worship. Bland prayer. Stale fellowship. Insipid evangelism. It all makes Christ *sick!*

Not just on Sunday. But Monday through Saturday, as well. Whenever our hearts, once fervent for Him, cool off into a state of lukewarmness, it makes Jesus Christ nauseated and sick to His stomach, making Him want to throw up.

It's all provoked by our sin of *lukewarmness*. The sin of being spiritually half in, half out. The sin of yawning in Christ's face. The sin of indifference toward His grace. The sin of being bored with the Christian life.

It makes Christ sick! He can't stomach it. Half-hearted devotion is absolutely revolting to Him.

This letter from Christ addresses the sin of lukewarmness. In scathing terms, Jesus warns that He will spew any lukewarm church from His mouth. This is a serious call to spiritual fervency, heart devotion, and holy zeal. Here is a solemn command to be *on fire* for Christ, not lukewarm.

THE SETTING

Laodicea was a city known for its affluence and prosperity. The worlds of commerce, manufacturing, and medicine all combined to make this a wealthy city.

Strategically located, Laodicea occupied a critical juncture on the major highway that ran from Ephesus in the west to Phrygia in the east. Also, the road from Pergamum and Sardis crossed this east-west route here in Laodicea. Situated in the fertile Lycus Valley, it formed a tri-city combination with Hierapolis, six miles to the north, and Colossae, ten miles east. Yet, it was definitely the hub, the judicial seat of the district.

When a great earthquake in 60 A.D. leveled this and other surrounding cities, Laodicea refused government aid to rebuild, while its citizens contributed heavily to help rebuild the other cities.

As the financial center of this part of the world, great sums of gold, silver, and Roman currency were kept on deposit here. It was to the banks of Laodicea that merchants and businessmen from all around came for financing for their business abroad.

Moreover, it was an important manufacturing hub. The local factories were famous for making a glossy, black wool that would become woven into expensive garments. Consequently, they were a fashion-conscious town with the latest styles.

Laodicea was also the seat of a famous medical center, boasting a leading school of medicine. A well-known eyesalve that helped cure eye diseases was developed by the physicians here.

This was a thriving, prosperous city!

The only drawback to Laodicea was its water supply. As the city grew, it became necessary to import water from outside sources. Consequently, underground aqueducts brought water into the city from Colossae and Hierapolis.

If Ephesus was like New York City, a bustling, cosmopolitan

seaport—and if Smyrna was like Atlanta, a growing, major metropolis—and if Pergamum was like Washington, D. C., the capital city
with political clout—and if Thyatira was like Detroit, a blue-collar,
hard-working, union town—and if Sardis was like Pittsburgh, a city
in decline—and if Philadelphia was like Little Rock, the land of
opportunity with an open door set before it—then Laodicea was like
Dallas. Growing. Prosperous. Affluent. Materialistic. High-fashion.
Self-sufficient. Self-made. A city on the rise.

THE SPEAKER

As with each letter, Jesus begins by revealing Himself to this church.
Only a startling self-disclosure of Himself could shake this church
out of its spiritual lethargy. So, here it is:

> "And to the angel of the church in Laodicea write: 'The Amen, the faith-
> ful and true Witness, the Beginning of the creation of God, says this: . . .'"
> (Revelation 3:14).

THE AMEN

First, Jesus calls Himself "the Amen." That means He is the embod-
iment of truth. All that He says is perfectly accurate and will be surely
accomplished. "Amen" implies certainty, veracity, and sincerity.
Christ's words are absolute, unchangeable truth.

This church needed to understand, first, that Jesus Christ is the
personification of truth. The ultimate reality. All other truth is mea-
sured by Him. His words are the divine standard. What He says is to
be utterly relied upon. His words are to be embraced without
reservation.

No doubt, Jesus identifies Himself this way to this church
because what He will say to them will be a jolt to their system.

THE WITNESS

Second, Jesus reveals Himself as "the faithful and true Witness." A
witness is someone who testifies to what is true. He speaks the truth
about what he has seen or heard. A faithful witness tells all he knows
and holds nothing back.

Jesus is "the faithful and true Witness" who will never misrepresent the truth. What Jesus sees in the life of this church, He will faithfully testify to them. He will neither exaggerate nor suppress any of the truth. He is fully reliable to communicate the truth, the whole truth, and nothing but the truth.

THE CREATOR

Third, Jesus is "the Beginning of the creation of God." This does not mean that He is the first created being. Such an idea is theological heresy. Rather, this means that Jesus is the Creator (*arche*) of all creation. He is the originator of all that there is. The leader of all creation. The One in charge. As the Creator, He is the ruler of all creation and possesses the right and prerogative of sovereign ownership.

Why would Jesus reveal Himself *this* way to *this* church? What is the significance of such a self-revelation to this church in Laodicea?

What Jesus has to say to this church will be so shocking, they will have difficulty believing His assessment. Christ's evaluation will be diametrically opposed to how they view themselves. They see themselves as rich, wealthy, and having need of nothing. But Jesus says, "No, quite the contrary. You are wretched, poor, miserable, blind, and naked." They must be reminded on the front end that Jesus is "the Amen, the faithful and true Witness" who cannot lie.

This church had gotten away from listening to God's Word. Instead, they were tuned in to the business world for their direction on how to run the church. A corporate model had become their goal, rather than the Word of Christ.

So, this worldly, materialistic church needed to be reminded that Jesus is the Creator of all that they were living for. Why live for "things" when you can live for the Creator?

THE STRENGTHS

Imagine the scene in Laodicea when this church is called together. The pastor comes with this letter from Jesus. First, copies of all the previous six letters are read, each containing a commendation for the strength of that church.

The letter to Ephesus is read. Then Smyrna, Pergamum,

Thyatira, Sardis, and Philadelphia. All containing praises. The members begin to anticipate what Jesus will commend them for. Will it be for their sizable giving? Will He praise them for their expanding programs?

The expectation level rises as their pastor reads, "To the angel of the church in Laodicea write . . ." But at this point, when they expect to hear the Lord's praise, they hear *nothing!*

No praise. No commendation. No affirmation.

Only silence.

Can't you feel the awkwardness of this moment? Remember, this is a vain church. Self-absorbed. Self-confident. Self-satisfied. Self-deceived. They actually expected to hear greater praise from Christ than He had for all the other churches.

Instead, they heard only the most stinging, scathing indictment that our Lord has for any of the churches. It was a devastating moment.

No strengths are listed!

Only sin.

THE SIN

The affluent culture of Laodicea was squeezing this church into its mold. So, Jesus must be straightforward with this church. What follows is the strongest and most scathing rebuke that Jesus will bring. So stinging are His words that there is no commendation. Only rebuke. His heart is too grieved to go beyond this complaint. Anything else would be superfluous to the core issue.

> *"I know your deeds, that you are neither cold nor hot; I would that you were cold or hot. So because you are lukewarm, and neither hot nor cold, I will spit you out of My mouth. Because you say, 'I am rich and have become wealthy, and have need of nothing,' and you do not know that you are wretched and miserable and poor and blind and naked" (Revelation 3:15-17).*

By saying, "I know your deeds," Jesus is saying, "I have a comprehensive and intimate knowledge of exactly where you are as a church." On the outside, this church looked eminently successful. Giving was up. Attendance was up. Activities were up. But Jesus saw with X-ray vision into the heart and soul of this church. With divine omniscience, he got a completely different read.

Here's what He saw: unveiled before His eyes was a church that was neither hot nor cold. They were something in between—lukewarm.

Jesus is saying, "I would rather that you be cold or hot. Anything but lukewarm. Get hot or get cold. Just don't be lukewarm!"

THE MEANING OF LUKEWARMNESS

What do these represent? What is it to be cold? Hot? Lukewarm?

First, *cold* means to be spiritually indifferent or apathetic. It pictures someone frozen in unbelief. Someone with zero interest in the kingdom of God. Such a person openly rejects the gospel. He is coolly indifferent toward Christ, even to the point of being openly hostile. Such a person is lost, unsaved, and separated from God.

Jesus said, "Because lawlessness is increased, most people's love will grow cold" (Matthew 24:12). Such hearts are cold toward the gospel. Unresponsive. Hardened. Frozen.

Second, *hot* pictures someone who is on fire for God. This person is fired up for spiritual things. He is inflamed with spiritual fervency for the kingdom of God. Here is someone heated to a boiling point. He is a flaming witness for Jesus Christ. Consumed with a red-hot passion, he has a burning zeal toward the Lord.

After His resurrection, Jesus appeared to two disciples on the road to Emmaus. After sharing intimate fellowship with Him, they said, "Were not our hearts burning within us while He was speaking to us . . . explaining the Scriptures to us?" (Luke 24:32). Their hearts were on fire with a glowing love for Him.

Third, *lukewarm* means to be half and half. Half cold, half hot. Blow hot, blow cold. Such a person is halfhearted toward Christ. A fence-straddler. Not wanting to commit one way or the other. One foot in the world, one foot in the church. Someone trying to play both ends into the middle. Someone who has enough religion to get him to church, yet not enough grace to change his life.

Who is this lukewarm person? Is this person saved or lost? What is his or her spiritual condition?

To answer that, some historical background will help our understanding of this passage. As we mentioned earlier, a major problem existed in Laodicea—an inadequate water supply. Their drinking water had to be brought in from nearby towns to meet their needs in Laodicea.

There were two outside sources for their water—Hierapolis and Colossae. An aqueduct brought some of their water six or seven miles from Colossae. This water was very cold and good for drinking. Conversely, Hierapolis was famous for its underground hot springs, much like Hot Springs, Arkansas. There, people would go to sit in the water for medicinal purposes to bring healing to their aching bodies.

But there was just one problem. By the time the hot water of Hierapolis was brought to Laodicea, it had cooled off along the way. It became adapted to the environment around it, or room temperature. By the time this hot water reached Laodicea, it was lukewarm and had lost its warm temperature.

Likewise, by the time the cool water came from Colossae, the same change occurred. No longer cool and refreshing to drink, it was insipidly lukewarm.

Both sources presented the same problem. Both water supplies had become lukewarm.

Consequently, there were two ways for their water to become lukewarm. The hot water of Hierapolis would become lukewarm, as would the cold water of Colossae. Both would become lukewarm. Either the hot water would cool off, or the cool water would warm up. By the time the water reached Laodicea, both water supplies had become room temperature.

The same was true spiritually in Laodicea. The church exactly paralleled this phenomenon. How could one be lukewarm in the church at Laodicea? The answer is, two different ways. One could be ice-cold and warm up to lukewarm, or one could be red-hot and cool off to lukewarm.

Let me explain.

Some believers in the church had once been on fire for God. These people were genuinely saved but had become worldly. Once burning for Christ, they had cooled off and adapted to the environment around them. They were now room temperature. Because of the world's influence, they had cooled off in their love for Jesus

Christ. Although truly converted to Christ, they had become carnal, worldly Christians. They were lukewarm.

But others in the church had never been born again. They professed to know Christ, but their hearts were unconverted. They had joined the church, but Christ had never joined them. They were cold, unsaved, and gradually adapted to the environment in the church. When in church, they warmed up to the glow and excitement of the true believers. They were lukewarm, yet never saved.

This is the greatest problem with many churches today. Unregenerate church members. Unconverted elders and deacons. Unredeemed pastors. Judases among the true disciples. Chaff among the wheat.

The church's first mission field must be its own membership. Many who say, "Lord, Lord" are on the broad road!

So, here, a major segment of the church was lukewarm. Some had been hot but were now lukewarm. Others had been cold but were also lukewarm. Within this same lukewarm group, some were saved, some were lost. Both looked alike. Both sounded alike. Some had been on fire but were now cooled off. Some had been cold but were now warmed up—not enough to be saved, just enough to get to church. Distinguishing between wheat and chaff is impossible to human eyes. So is distinguishing between the lukewarm saved and the lukewarm lost.

Speaking directly to the problem, Jesus says, "I know your deeds, that you are neither cold nor hot. You're right here in the middle. You're lukewarm. I wish that you were cold or hot."

THE CURSE OF LUKEWARMNESS

Why would Jesus say, "I wish that you were cold or hot"? Why would He rather that they be cold than lukewarm? Three important reasons need to be noted.

The first deals with our *relationship with Christ*. The most difficult person to be converted is a church member who thinks he or she is saved, but has never been born again. Such a person fails to see his or her need to be saved. Because he or she is a church member, he or she assumes that he or she is going to heaven—but he or she is not! Such persons' names are written on the church roll, but not in the Lamb's book of life. They have had an encounter with a pastor or evangelist, but not with Jesus Christ.

John Walvoord writes, "There is no one farther from the truth in Christ than the one who makes an idle profession without real faith. How many church members are far from God, yet by their membership in a professing church, have been lulled to sleep into a false security? No one has been harder to reach for Christ than the religionist. Far easier to win the harlots and publicans than to win the Pharisees and Sadducees."

Thus, Jesus said, "I'd rather you be cold! If you're lost, it would be better that you not think that you are saved. I would rather you be all-out against Me. Then you would not have a false assumption that you are going to heaven. At least when one is ice-cold, he or she *knows* that he or she is lost."

No one can be saved until he or she first knows that he or she is lost. As long as one is lukewarm, a person will falsely assume he or she is saved when, in reality, he or she is not.

Could this be you? Are you trusting in your church membership or good life to get you to heaven? It will not. Jesus told Nicodemus, one of the most righteous and religious men in all Israel, "Unless one is born again, he cannot see the kingdom of God" (John 3:3).

Such a false security makes God *sick!*

The second reason deals with our *influence for Christ*. The negative effect of a lukewarm Christian upon unbelievers is devastating. A lukewarm believer is the worst advertisement for Christianity. This tepid person keeps the one who is cold from coming to the flames of the gospel of Jesus Christ.

When a lost man sees the lukewarm Christian who is worldly, he reasons, "Why do I even need to be saved? If this is what being a Christian is all about, I don't need Christianity. He's no different than me."

That's why Jesus says, "Listen, I would rather you be cold—out and out against Me—than be lukewarm, because others are making a decision about Me by the way you live your life."

Lukewarmness makes God *sick!*

The third reason deals with our *worship of Christ*. Jesus says, "I would rather you be out and out against Me than to be lukewarm, because lukewarmness is blasphemy." G. Campbell Morgan said,

"Lukewarmness is the worst form of blasphemy." The lukewarm Christian says, "Oh yeah, I believe in Jesus Christ as my Lord and Savior. But He's just not much to get excited about. Christ just bores me."

This is blasphemy! It would be better to not even be a believer in Christ than to believe in Him only to yawn in His face. "Yeah, you're no big deal, Jesus!"

To such a benign believer, Jesus says, "Get hot, get cold, or get out! Because you are lukewarm and neither hot nor cold, I will spit you out of my mouth." Lukewarmness makes God sick! Strong language, isn't it? In fact, very crude language.

To such lukewarm believers, Jesus says, "I spit you out of my mouth." This means, literally, to vomit, to throw up. God is saying, "When you are indifferent and lukewarm about Me, you make Me sick to My stomach."

Does that shock you? It ought to. Let that settle down in your heart. God is not some kind of impassioned accountant in heaven, simply making marks in His divine ledger, running the universe in a cold, calculated way. He is Someone with deep emotions, passionate zeal, and a loving heart. He wants to have a personal, intimate relationship with us.

God has loved us and has given His Son to die on the cross. But when we turn our backs on Him, we callously yawn in His face. To which He says, "You make me want to throw up! Barf! Puke! You are utterly obnoxious to me! You bring a sickening effect to the very pit of my stomach. You make me want to regurgitate!"

Lukewarmness triggers a sharp, violent reaction from God. A lack of heart is utterly repugnant to Him.

When we drink tea, we want it to be cold or hot. Just not lukewarm. Iced tea is good. Hot tea is fine. But lukewarm is offensive. Anything but lukewarm. Lukewarm is nauseating. Disturbing. Insipid. Tepid.

Jesus says, "Get off the fence. Come out and out for Me. Or be out and out against Me. Just don't be indifferent. Get hot, get cold, or get out. Lukewarmness makes Me sick to my stomach."

Strong words from a passionate Lord.

Could that be you? Does this describe your heart? Are you lukewarm? Could you be indifferent? Are you apathetic? Is the glow gone? Is your passion missing?

THE CAUSE OF LUKEWARMNESS

What is the *cause* of this indifference toward God? Why were many in Laodicea lukewarm? How could they fall to this insipid status?

Jesus exposes the problem when He says, "Because you say, 'I am rich, and have become wealthy, and have need of nothing'" (verse 17). They were plagued with worldliness, materialism, and a smug self-sufficiency.

Here were people absorbed with the things of the world. Climbing the social ladder. Advancing their career. Getting ahead in the world. The latest fashion style. Buying things. They lived for these pursuits.

Their worldly successes bred a smug self-sufficiency. With a haughty complacency, they thought, "We're wired for whatever we need. We're rich and wealthy. We must be doing everything right because God is blessing us. We're prosperous, so we must be right with God. We don't need anything because we've got big bank accounts. Why pray? God has already blessed us."

Pointedly, Jesus—"the Amen, the faithful and true Witness"—had to say to this shop-'til-you-drop bunch, "You do not know that you are wretched, miserable, poor, blind, and naked." In other words, Jesus' assessment was 180 degrees different than their estimate. They couldn't have been any more wrong about themselves.

They thought they were O.K. But Jesus said they were K.O.'d.

Simply put, this church didn't know that they didn't know. It's one thing to be ignorant. It's another thing to be ignorant of your ignorance. This is double jeopardy!

We have heard the story of the emperor who wore no clothes. He paid large sums of money to two clothiers to make him the finest clothes money could buy. But, playing a game of deception, they put nothing on him and told him he was wearing the finest robe in the kingdom. The vain king believed their lie and proudly walked around his castle naked, pretending to be well-dressed. Everyone was too fearful to tell the king the truth.

Until one little boy stated what everyone else knew but were afraid to say. So he blurted out, "The emperor has no clothes on!"

In a moment, the game was over. Embarrassed, the king ran for cover.

Spiritually speaking, that's how these believers came to church. Naked. Undressed. In their birthday suits. But thinking that they were well-dressed and smartly-attired.

They paraded into church wearing their fashionable clothes and dropped large sums of money into the offering plate, all the while thinking that they were spiritually adorned with garments of righteousness. Yet, Jesus said, "You think you're well-attired, but you're naked! You think you're getting ahead in the world, but you're broke! You think you're something special, but you're wretched. You actually may think you're happy, but behind your plastic smiles you're miserable."

It is amazing we can be so deceived! It's when we think that we've got our act together spiritually that we've lost it. Whenever we think we have no need is when our need is the greatest.

Our greatest need is to see our need. Without a proper selfknowledge, we have no hunger for God.

Could this be you? Honestly, before God, where are you? Are you lukewarm? Are you hot, cold, or indifferent toward the things of God? Where are you?

Maybe you are hot and on fire for God. That's great! Maybe there is a zeal and a passion and a spiritual heartbeat about you.

On the other hand, perhaps you are half in and half out. Maybe saved, maybe lost. Nobody can tell either way.

Are you lukewarm about the Scriptures? Is there still a burning hunger for God's Word that is growing and spreading? Is your heart set on fire by the Scriptures? Or do you read the Bible in a mechanical, academic, routine way? Do you read the Word and remain flat, detached, and sterile? Do you even read it at all?

Are you lukewarm about prayer? Is there a burning, passionate zeal in your heart to be in the presence of God? Is there an anticipation to be alone with the Lord in prayer? Is there a life-changing dynamic about your prayer life? Or are you bored to death with prayer? Are your prayers just rote, routine, and mundane? When you get on your knees, is the thrill gone? Do you even pray at all?

Are you lukewarm about witnessing? Are you excited about sharing your faith in Jesus Christ? Are you gladly looking for opportunities to witness for Him? Do you feel you can't hold yourself back to talk about Christ? Or are you just lukewarm and inconspicuously blending in with the environment around you? Would you just as soon not get involved in someone else's life? Are you no longer burdened for the lost? Do you even care that lost people are going to an eternal, fiery hell?

Are you lukewarm about serving Christ? Is there a spiritual heartbeat in your life to give yourself away to others? Do you still feel an excitement about serving God that energizes you? Or are you just cranking out your service because you have to? Has your ministry lost its passion? Have you become indifferent and callous in serving others?

What is the temperature of your heart? You may be lukewarm because you have never been born again. If so, you are indifferent because you have never had open-heart surgery. You need to ask God to take away your old, cold heart and give you a new, flaming heart for Him. Maybe you have joined a church and you attend. Your spiritual pulse warms up a bit when you hear the choir sing or the Scriptures preached. But the truth is, you have never come all the way to Christ to be born again. No wonder you're lukewarm.

THE SOLUTION

Jesus now gives the correction for lukewarmness. First, Jesus will address lukewarm church members who know Christ but have cooled off. Then He will speak to church members who are lost and have never been on fire for God. So, Jesus will first address the saved (verses 18-19), then the lost (verse 20). Both groups are lukewarm. One needs revival, the other needs regeneration. Both need to become fired-up for Christ.

A WORD TO BELIEVERS

Jesus begins by speaking to lukewarm church members who are genuine believers. To these self-sufficient saints, He says:

> *"I advise you to buy from Me gold refined by fire, that you may become rich, and white garments that you may clothe yourself, and that the shame of your nakedness may not be revealed, and eyesalve to anoint your eyes,*

that you may see. Those whom I love, I reprove and discipline; be zealous
therefore, and repent" (Revelation 3:18-19).

There is a touch of irony here. Jesus is speaking to externally conscious, materialistic believers who are more excited about buying and shopping than about worshiping and praying. They are more passionate about worldly things than the spiritual.

To these Jesus says, "I advise you to buy from Me." He's saying, "You need to do business with Me. You need what only I can give you. Instead of stockpiling material things, you need to acquire from Me spiritual things. You cannot buy My treasures at the store."

There is a deep irony about all three of these commodities—gold, white garments, and eyesalve. Laodicea was famous for having all three of these in abundance. That part of the world came to Laodicea to buy these valuable items. Yet, Jesus says to those people that they need to buy the same from Him!

Obviously, our Lord is making reference to spiritual realities that each of these products represent. They must come and buy from Him spiritual gold, heavenly garments, and true eyesalve. These are invaluable possessions that money cannot buy. Only repentance can complete this transaction.

First, they need to buy "gold refined by fire." This is pure gold with all the dross removed through the refining process. "Gold" refers to what is most valuable and costly. That is our faith in God. Our faith is often compared to gold refined in the fires of trials (James 1:2-4; Proverbs 17:3). Jesus invites these believers to come to Him for a deeper faith that is pure in its fidelity toward Him.

Second, they need to buy from Christ "white garments." This clothing refers to the righteous deeds of the saints (Revelation 19:8). This admonition means to recommit one's life to obedient deeds of righteousness.

They also need to buy eyesalve. This refers to an anointing of the eyes by the illuminating ministry of the Holy Spirit. Only the Spirit can open our eyes to see God, spiritual truth, and ourselves. The Holy Spirit must remove self-deception and give spiritual vision. Christ is saying, "You need the ministry of the Holy Spirit to open your eyes, so you will see how naked, blind, and wretched you really are. Until you see your sin, you will never repent."

Jesus says, "Come to Me and buy what you desperately need. Come surrender your life to Me, and give Me your whole heart. Receive from Me that which you really need—a genuine faith in God, a renewed heart to obey Him, and a discernment of spiritual matters."

What will happen if they don't do business with Him? Jesus warns that He will discipline them. He says, "Those whom I love, I reprove and discipline" (verse 19).

These verses are clearly addressed to Christians. God only disciplines His own children (Hebrews 12:5-11). As a father, I don't discipline my neighbor's children, nor the kids down the block. I only discipline my own children. Similarly, Jesus says, "Those whom I love, I reprove and discipline."

Jesus loves His own—even when they are disobedient. The word here translated "love" is not *agape*, meaning a volitional choice of the will to love. Surprisingly, it is *phileo*, which we normally assess as a lesser love. It's a love of feelings, affections, and emotions. In this context though, it is the strongest word that Christ could have used.

Jesus has already opened His heart and revealed His disturbing feelings about them. "You make me sick." At the same time, He also wants them to know that He still loves them with the deepest yearnings of His heart. The one who can grieve you the most is, strangely, the one you love the most. Those dearest to your heart can most easily break your heart. Jesus says, "I still love (*phileo*) you from the very depths of My heart, from the pit of My stomach, from the core of My being. I feel a deep, passionate love for you. I still love you. Turn back to Me."

The word "zealous" (verse 19) means to be on fire. It pictures something reaching the boiling point. He's saying, "Turn your life around, and get on fire for Me again. Rekindle your heart toward Me before I have to discipline you."

Maybe you're a Christian, but your passion is gone. Jesus says to you, "Come, resubmit your life afresh to Me. Turn away from the things of the world. Repent of your preoccupation with your career, your house, your family, your recreations, or whatever else. Get refocused on Me. Repent and be zealous."

A WORD TO UNBELIEVERS

Jesus now addresses lukewarm church members who were *not* genuine believers. These people profess Christ, but do *not* possess Him. They are tares among the wheat. Once cold, they have drawn closer to the fire. But they have not come all the way to Christ. They are lukewarm, lost church members.

To these unregenerate, Jesus says:

> *"Behold, I stand at the door and knock; if any one hears My voice and opens the door, I will come in to him, and will dine with him, and he with Me" (verse 20).*

What a great invitation!

This door represents the entrance into one's heart. It is either opened or closed when Christ approaches. When closed, He stands knocking, seeking entrance. He's been there all along. He is patiently knocking. Trying to get their attention. This is the convicting ministry of the Holy Spirit, pounding on our hearts, seeking entrance for Christ. But these people have been so preoccupied with worldly pursuits that they haven't even heard His persistent knocking.

Jesus could knock the door down if He wanted. Yet, He desires to be invited. That's our human responsibility. We must respond by faith and open our hearts to receive Jesus Christ. As an act of our wills, we must personally invite Christ to come live within our hearts. We must receive Him as our Lord and Savior. "As many as received Him, to them He gave the right to become children of God, even to those who believe in His name" (John 1:12).

Salvation is more than the mere intellectual knowledge of facts about Christ. We must open our hearts and invite Him to come in. That requires our repentance and faith.

If we will invite Christ, He promises to take up residence in our lives. Jesus says, "If any one hears My voice and opens the door, I will come in to him." What a promise! The God of heaven and earth will come live within our lowly hearts.

You can't get any closer than that! Christianity is an intimate, personal relationship with Christ. Salvation is more than getting man out of hell and into heaven. It is also getting Christ out of heaven and into man.

When Christ comes into our lives, He does so to "dine" with us. Eating a meal pictures close fellowship with another person. It represents sitting down across the table from someone and fellowshiping with that person. Visiting. Talking. Listening. Encouraging one another. Intimate friendship.

That's what a personal relationship with Christ is like. We can pour out our hearts to Him and tell Him anything we want. We can share with Him our deepest concerns and greatest needs. What a privilege.

Have you opened your heart and received Jesus Christ? If not, why not now? You're not saved by merely knowing some intellectual facts about Christ. Nor are you saved by coming to church or doing enough good works. Salvation means inviting Jesus Christ to come live within your heart. It is experiencing a personal, life-changing relationship with Him.

THE SUCCESS

Jesus concludes with a great promise of hope to His true followers. Jesus says:

> *"He who overcomes, I will grant to him to sit down with Me on My throne, as I also overcame and sat down with My Father on His throne"* *(Revelation 3:21).*

An overcomer is one who does not fall prey to the lukewarmness addressed in this letter. He is one who overcomes lukewarmness. Sure, we all fall into a season of lukewarmness from time to time. But an overcomer won't remain insipid. He will overcome his spiritual indifference by rekindling his heart toward Christ.

Overcomers are promised the privilege of sitting down with Christ on His throne. If that promise was not stated here in the Bible, I would say such a statement is blasphemy. But that's what Jesus promises us. We *will* sit down with Him on His throne in the sense of sharing in His eternal reign.

With this promise, Jesus looks forward to the time of His second coming. When He returns, He will usher in His kingdom on earth. At that time, our Lord will surround Himself with those who have been faithful to Him in this lifetime. All who have served Christ in this lifetime will be assigned places of special responsibility and will sit on the thrones to share in His millennial rule.

In 1993 a new administration moved into the White House in Washington, D.C. Guess who the President placed into his Cabinet? He surrounded himself with those who had been faithful to him over the years. His trusted devotees have been given key Cabinet positions. Some of his highest-ranking officials today were unknown nobodies yesterday. But they have now been elevated to serve in high positions in the new administration. They hold seats of great responsibility simply because over the years they have been faithful to the one who is now President.

That's exactly what will happen when Christ returns. He will inaugurate His kingdom and delegate to His overcomers key positions of authority. A lot of nobodies today like you and me will be promoted to key positions of leadership in the kingdom to come. One day the saints will rule and reign with Christ on the earth (Matthew 19:28; 1 Corinthians 6:3; Revelation 20:4).

With such a glorious future before us, how could we possibly be lukewarm toward Him? If He suffered, bled, and died on Calvary's cross and purchased us with His own blood, how can we be indifferent toward Him?

We can overcome because He overcame. Christ overcame through His sacrificial death. By means of His obedience, He was raised and is seated at the Father's right hand in heaven. Our obedience to God enables us to overcome as well. It is through our obedience that we will one day be rewarded to sit in heavenly places.

THE SUMMONS

Jesus now concludes this seventh and final letter as He has each of the previous six letters. He concludes with a passionate, personal appeal to hear the message of this letter—and to act upon it.

> *"He who has an ear, let him hear what the Spirit says to the churches"*
> *(Revelation 3:22).*

To hear and not to obey is not to hear at all. We must take to heart the message of this letter to the church at Laodicea. Christ is speaking to each and every one of us. Let us truly hear what He says.

The message is clear. Lukewarmness toward Christ is a gross sin against our Lord. Our spiritual apathy toward Jesus causes Him greatest grief and heartbreak. We must constantly read the thermostat of our heart. When we cool off and become lukewarm, decisive steps must be taken immediately to raise the temperature of our spiritual passion.

Perhaps this is our greatest need. Could it be that the greatest need of the church is to get *fired up* for Christ?

That's what Jesus says. We must rekindle the spiritual passion within our hearts for Him. That's at the very core of what the church is to be. We are called to be a body of believers deeply in love with Christ.

When the world sees the reality of our love for Christ, the gospel message we share is made believable. One life on fire for Christ is worth more than a library full of arguments. The world is waiting to see the reality of our love for Him.

A church once caught on fire. The entire neighborhood ran down the street to see the church aflame. The fire was so hot that there was no hope of saving the buildings.

Present among the bystanders was the town atheist. He was known for his unbelief and his cynical attacks on the church. As he stood there watching the church burn, one of the members saw him and sarcastically said, "What are you doing here? I never thought I'd see *you* at church."

The atheist replied, "You'll have to excuse me. But I've never seen a church on fire before."

I think that's what the world needs to see. A church on fire. Not lukewarm and indifferent. But full of members with a red-hot love for Jesus Christ.

That's what the world needs to see.

A church *on fire!*

CONCLUSION:

THE LAWS OF REVIVAL

XI

THIS IS NO TIME TO PLAY CHURCH

Revelation 2–3

PLAYING CHURCH CAN BE FUN.

It all depends on who's playing it.

On a family vacation years ago, my wife, Anne, my children, and I decided to have our own church service on Sunday morning. My son, James, at that time only five years old, was the preacher, imitating me. His twin brother, Andrew, mimicked the Pastor of Worship at our church. Anne, my daughter Grace Anne, one and a half, and I formed the congregation.

The living room was our sanctuary. An end table, the pulpit. A love seat and sofa, our pews. And a candy tray, the collection plate.

To start the service, Andrew led us in singing "Amazing Grace." As he orchestrated the music, his arms waved frantically in the air—like a man fighting off a swarm of bees. Following our singing, James stood up behind the table, opened his Bible, and preached the story of the conversion of Zaccheus. Billy Graham could not have done a better job.

At the close of the sermon, James gave an invitation for us to be saved. When none of us responded, he publicly called out Grace Anne—*by name*, no less—to come forward and be saved. Trust me, James did *not* learn this technique from me. Although, I must admit, I have been tempted to name a few names in some sermons.

Willing to do anything to please her older brother, Grace Anne walked forward, knelt over the coffee table, and was "saved." But as James was concluding the service, Andrew hopped back up—now standing directly in front of his brother—to lead us in another verse of "Amazing Grace." No way was he going to let his brother have the last word.

So, we sang again. But before Andrew could dismiss the service, James stood back up—right in front of his brother—to preach another sermon. Which he did—the *exact same* sermon. No way was he going to let Andrew have the last word.

Again James extended an invitation for us to come to the front. And again Grace Anne was called out by name to come forward to be saved. Which she did—her *second* conversion in *five* minutes!

As James was ready to dismiss us—you guessed it!—Andrew stood back up. And the whole cycle started over again.

This jockeying for position went on for another six or seven rounds. Neither boy was willing to let his brother have the final word.

Finally, when I realized that this "tag-team" ministry could go on indefinitely, I took over the pulpit and pronounced the benediction to end this marathon. I had to—Grace Anne was getting too tired walking forward to continue any longer.

Playing church can be fun.

It all depends on who's playing it.

With children, it can be lots of fun. It can be an enjoyable family experience. But with adults, playing church can be *deadly*. Sad to say, too many adults are doing just that—playing church. Unfortunately, they are not on vacation with their kids. They are in the house of the living God to worship the risen Christ.

Tragically, these adults are just going through the empty motions of playing church. They are playacting. Pretending. Role-playing. Dressing the part. Playing oneupmanship. Following a rehearsed script. Turning in Academy Award-winning performances.

That's precisely what the word *hypocrite* means. In the ancient world, this Greek word meant one who walked onto a stage, put on a mask, and played a part according to a script. While on stage, he pretended to be someone he wasn't. But once the play was over, he walked off the stage, took off his mask, and resumed his true identity. That's a hypocrite.

That's precisely what Jesus called the Pharisees of His day (Matthew 6:5). They had mastered the game of playing church. They knew how to look and sound the part. When they fasted, they put on a gloomy face. When they gave, they blew a trumpet. When they prayed, they acted out a performance!

The people were spellbound. These performances were absolutely captivating. Trouble was, it was all a game. The Pharisees were hiding behind masks of pretense. Sound familiar?

Two thousand years have elapsed, and little has changed. Churches today are still full of playactors. They come Sunday by Sunday and put on their masks at the front door. The pastor follows his script, and the people play out their roles. They say their rehearsed lines perfectly. All the while hiding behind a mask. And when church is over, they step off the stage, take their masks off, and go back to being who they really are.

Now, *that's* playing church!

I am all too familiar with this stage production. As a pastor, I have worked very closely with one church for the past thirteen years. Amid the true worshipers, I see the bit players. Likewise, I have traveled from coast to coast with the Billy Graham Evangelistic Association and have spoken to thousands of pastors and church leaders. And wherever I go, I see the same.

Adults are playing church.

Why do grown-ups pretend? Why do adults go through the empty motions of such a masquerade?

Simple. They don't have the real thing. In the absence of a growing knowledge of God, void of the fullness of the Spirit's power, they put on their masks and parrot their lines. Anything to look the part. Anything to sound spiritual.

Worst, in the absence of any real spiritual power, pastors are turning to the latest gimmicks and current fads to generate church growth and hold their "audiences." Church leaders are desperately trying to jump on the latest bandwagon to fill the vacuum. But all the while, they neglect the *real* thing—a genuine work of God in the hearts of their people.

WE NEED REVIVAL!

Quite simply, the need of the hour is revival. We need the real thing—a spiritual awakening to sweep through our slumbering congregations and put us back on our knees before the living Lord.

The word *revival* conjures up different pictures to different people. If you have lived in the South as I do, a *revival* means a week-long series of meetings at the church held by a powerful evangelist wearing a three-piece white suit. Each of these "revival" meetings are primarily designed to reach unbelievers for Christ.

That's all fine and good, but that's not what revival is. Evangelism is not revival. That's *regeneration*. Revival is strengthening *believers* in the church. Reaching the unsaved is the by-product of revival. Revival is a sovereign work of God in His own people, bringing back to full spiritual fervor the hearts of believers that are now dormant and dull.

J. I. Packer defines revival as "a visitation of God which brings to life Christians who have been sleeping and restores a deep sense of God's near presence and holiness. All this ushers in a vivid sense of sin and a profound exercise of heart in repentance, praise, and love with an evangelistic overflow."

Stephen Olford writes, "Revival is that strange, sovereign work of God in which He visits the people—restoring, reanimating, and releasing them into the fullness of His blessing. Such a divine intervention will issue in evangelism, though, in the first instance, it is a work of God in the church and among individual believers."

Charles Finney, the revivalist of the early nineteenth century, defined revival as "a new beginning of obedience." Simply put, it is a new humility. A new closeness to God. A new passion for Christ. A new love for God. A new desire for holiness. A new filling with the Holy Spirit.

That's what revival is.

It is a sovereign and mysterious work of God, just as the new birth is. It cannot be coerced, nor manipulated. It is a supernatural work of God in His church that restores her lost purity, devotion, and power. Revival restores to full health the spiritual life that is already present in the church. It is the renewing, purifying, replenishing work of the Holy Spirit in the life of the church.

In reality, revival is a time of divine visitation. It is an invasion from heaven that manifests the presence and power of God in the church. It ushers in a renewed, conscious awareness of God's awesome holiness that produces holiness in the church. Now, *that's* the real thing!

Probably the best definition of revival found anywhere in the Bible is contained in the letter to the church at Sardis. Let me refresh your memory. Jesus writes:

> *"I know your deeds, that you have a name that you are alive, but you are dead. Wake up, and strengthen the things which remain, which were about to die . . ." (Revelation 3:1-2).*

This church was dead! That does not mean that they were lost or separated from God, as Ephesians 2:1 says. Instead, these men and women in Sardis were genuinely converted to Christ. Their deadness meant that they had lost their spiritual passion and fervency for Christ. They were flat and devoid of spiritual power. By outward appearances, they looked religious and sounded pious. But in reality, they were dead.

Jesus called them to wake up. That's what revival is—it is a *spiritual awakening* of those who are lethargic toward Christ. It is a sleeping church—unconscious, unresponsive, unexcited—*waking up* to the presence of God and returning to full spiritual vitality. It's waking up to Jesus Christ and allowing Him to strengthen what spiritual life remains.

How can we wake up? How can we have revival in the church and in our lives? How can we stop playing church and have the real thing?

I want to conclude this book by surveying the seven letters to the seven churches. There are several truths that run through all seven letters—or, at least, most of them—that deserve our attention. Here are the common threads that run through all the letters that weave the tapestry of revival.

THE SIX LAWS OF REVIVAL

Hopefully, we're in agreement that we need revival. So, practically speaking, *how* do we restore our spiritual heartbeat for Christ? *How* do we escape the deadly game of playing church? Here's how to have a spiritual awakening.

1. THE LAW OF PROCLAMATION

Revival begins with the ministry of the Word of God. It begins with the preaching and teaching of the Word of God to the church in the power of the Holy Spirit. Why is that? Because the Scriptures are full of the life of God (1 Peter 1:23; John 6:63). And if we are to have God's life within the church revived, then God's Word—which is *"living"* and *"active"* (Hebrews 4:12)—must invade our lives. Like produces like. The Word of God revives the life of God in His people.

So, we are not surprised that each of the seven letters begins the same way. They begin with a call for the proclamation of God's Word. "To the angel of the church in Ephesus *write* . . ." (Revelation 2:1), "To the angel of the church in Smyrna *write* . . ." (2:8), "To the angel of the church in Pergamum *write* . . ." (2:12), "To the angel of the church in Thyatira *write* . . ." (2:18), "To the angel of the church in Sardis *write* . . ." (3:1), "To the angel of the church in Philadelphia *write* . . ." (3:7), and "To the angel of the church in Laodicea *write* . . ." (3:14). The emphasis is upon the communication and proclamation of the written Word of God.

In each case, the pastor of the church is told to communicate the written Word of Christ to His congregation. That's where revival begins. It begins when the pastor and the spiritual leadership of the church preach and teach the Word of God.

D. L. Moody said, "The best way to start a revival is to build a fire in the pulpit."

Christ promises to bring a great spiritual blessing to the church where God's Word is preached. Earlier John wrote:

> *Blessed is he who reads and those who hear the words of the prophecy, and heed the things which are written in it (Revelation 1:3).*

This verse pictures the public gathering, or worship service, of the church. The Word of God is to be read by the pastor ("he who reads"). And it is to be heard and obeyed by the entire church ("those who hear . . . and heed the things which are written in it").

It is the Word of God—preached, heard, applied, and obeyed—that brings revival to the hearts of God's people.

That's precisely what Psalm 119 tells us. Revival comes when the Word of God invades our lives, searches our hearts, and produces holiness. The psalmist says, "Revive *me* according to Thy word" (verse 25). He pleaded, "*Revive me* in Thy ways" (verse 37). "Thy ways" is a synonym for the Word of God because it points out the way we are to take. Again he says, "*Revive me* through Thy righteousness" (verse 40). "Thy righteousness" is another synonym for God's Word because it defines right and wrong. Also, "I will never forget Thy precepts, for by them Thou hast *revived me*" (verse 93). Finally, "*Revive me* according to Thy word" (verse 154).

Likewise, each of the seven letters ends with the same maxim: "He who has an ear, let him hear what the Spirit says to the churches" (Revelation 2:7, 11, 17, 29; 3:6, 13, 22). Revival occurs when God's Word is preached, heard, and, by the Spirit's ministry of illumination and conviction, applied to our lives.

If there is to be a revival in our churches, it must begin in our pulpits. Pastors must return to bold, biblical preaching of holy Scripture (2 Timothy 3:16—4:5). That was the plea of Charles Haddon Spurgeon over one hundred years ago.

> We want again Luthers, Calvins, Bunyans, Whitefields, men fit to mark eras, whose names breathe terror in our foemen's ears. We have dire need of such. Whence will they come to us? They are the gifts of Jesus Christ to the Church, and will come in due time. He has power to give us back again a golden age of preachers, a time as fertile of great divines and mighty ministers as was the Puritan age, and when the good old truth is once more preached by men whose lips are touched as with a live coal from off the altar, this shall be the instrument in the hand of the Spirit for bringing about a great and thorough revival of religion in the land.
>
> I do not look for any other means of converting men beyond the simple preaching of the gospel and the opening of men's ears to hear it. The moment the Church of God shall despise the pulpit, God will despise her. It has been through the ministry that the Lord has always been pleased to revive and bless His Churches.

Many things today have been offered to replace biblical preaching. Some of them—musicals, Christian talk shows, movies, and drama—have a place in the church. But they must never be allowed to replace the centrality of the pulpit. The need of the hour is for powerful, Spirit-energized preaching.

John MacArthur writes, "A holy man who is gifted to preach by the Spirit of God and prepared in the Word of God has no equal in a power presentation of the truth." Think about that! God only had one Son, and He made Him a preacher (Mark 1:14).

If we are to have revival, we must return again to biblical preaching that exalts Christ, exposes sin, encourages hope, builds faith, and calls for a verdict. It is the proclamation of the Word that prepares the way for revival.

Preach the Word!

2. THE LAW OF EXALTATION

Only one kind of preaching initiates revival. The kind that exalts the supremacy of Christ in the life of the church. We must have a high view of Christ. A work of God in the church can run no deeper than the height with which Christ is exalted. Our eyes must behold the glories of our enthroned Lord.

In each of these seven letters, there follows a self-description of Christ given by Jesus Himself. Before we see anything else, we must see Him. Each church's greatest need is to see their Sovereign Lord. The life of the church can grow no higher than their knowledge of Him. We must be overwhelmed with a high view of Jesus Christ and obsessed with His glory.

A. W. Tozer writes:

> To regain her lost power, the Church must see heaven opened and have a transforming vision of God. But the God we must see is not the unitarian God who is having such a run of popularity today, whose chief claim to men's attention is His ability to bring them success in their various undertakings. . . . The God we must learn to know is the Majesty in the heavens, God the Father Almighty, Maker of heaven and earth, the only wise God, our Savior.

Consequently, each church is given a unique revelation of Christ's majesty. Each description is different than the one He gives to the other churches. That's because Jesus uniquely revealed Himself to each church in a way specifically designed to meet the most glaring spiritual need of that congregation.

So, to Ephesus Jesus revealed Himself as the One who holds the seven stars and who walks among the lampstands (Revelation 2:1). To Smyrna, He is the First and the Last, the One who was dead and has come back to life (2:8). To Pergamum, the One who has the sharp, two-edged sword (2:12). To Thyatira, the Son of God who has blazing eyes and burnished feet (2:18). To Sardis, He holds the seven spirits and seven stars (3:1). To Philadelphia, the holy and true One who possesses the key of David (3:7). And to Laodicea, the Amen, the faithful and true Witness, the Beginning of the creation of God (3:14).

Herein is the second key to revival. A spiritual awakening occurs when we lift high our exalted Lord and see His majestic Lordship. It occurs when we grow in the personal knowledge of Christ (2 Peter 3:18) and behold His glory in greater and fuller ways. This is the church's *greatest* need—to see the unrivaled, sovereign supremacy of Jesus Christ.

This awesome revelation comes primarily through the *Christ-honoring* preaching of God's Word, through *Christ-exalting* corporate worship, through *Christ-focused* praying in Jesus' name, and through the *Christ-centered* fellowship of Spirit-filled believers. Every church must major in the glory of our ascended, exalted Lord Jesus Christ.

Too many churches today offer a man-centered message that is geared toward our felt needs. But our greatest need is to see the glory of Christ.

Are you aware of your deepest need to behold the majesty of Christ? What emphasis of His divine character does He need to impress upon your heart? Perhaps His near presence among the lampstands? Or His omniscience with fiery eyes? Perhaps His power to send the Holy Spirit? Or His holiness as the infinitely pure One? Which emphasis is most needed in your church? Which is most needed in your life?

Open your eyes. Lift high the name of Christ! See His exalted Lordship! Then revival will begin to flood your heart.

3. THE LAW OF CONTINUATION

The third law of revival requires that we continue walking in love, faith, and good deeds. That's the next feature of each of the seven letters—all except the last one. Following a self-description of Christ comes a commendation by Christ to continue in holiness. In each instance, Jesus affirms what the church was doing right. Jesus encourages each church to continue faithfully in those areas in which they are on target.

What is it that Jesus approves of in any church or believer? What is it that Jesus wants us to continue pursuing?

A condensing of the seven letters reveals that Christ desires, first, *hard work*. To Ephesus He said, "I know your deeds and your toil and perseverance" (Revelation 2:2). When our Lord looks down from heaven and sees selfless, sacrificial ministry, He says, "I like that!"

After all, Jesus Himself came not to be served, but to serve. The Word became flesh in order that He might give His life a ransom for many (Mark 10:45). The church is to be like her Lord, constantly giving to meet the needs of others.

Second, Jesus wants *holiness* in His churches. He commends those in Sardis who "have not soiled their garments" (Revelation 3:4) because they have kept themselves morally pure—mentally, physically, spiritually. Worldliness quenches the fires of revival.

To Ephesus He says, "You cannot endure evil men . . . you hate the deeds of the Nicolaitans, which I also hate" (Revelation 2:2, 6). He commends them for exercising church discipline and for removing sinful members who are living lives of known disobedience. Jesus said, "I don't like it either. I am standing with you as you stand against sin."

Third, Jesus commends *doctrinal integrity*. At Ephesus, they "put to the test those who call themselves apostles, and they are not, and you found them to be false" (Revelation 2:2). He commends those in Thyatira for not holding to the teaching of Jezebel, for not delving into "the deep things of Satan" (Revelation 2:24).

Revival requires that every effort be made to maintain purity of doctrine. False teaching hinders the work of the Spirit.

Fourth, Jesus commends the churches for their *faithful witness*. In fact, more than anything else, Jesus draws attention to their testimony for Him. Ephesus endured for Christ's name's sake. To Smyrna Jesus said, "The devil is about to throw some of you into prison. . . . Be faithful until death." To Pergamum He said, "You hold fast My name, and did not deny My faith." To Philadelphia He wrote, "You have kept My word, and have not denied My name" (cf. Revelation 2:3, 10, 13; 3:8). Standing up for Christ and confessing Him to a godless society inflames our hearts with deeper love for Christ.

In which of these areas of your Christian life are you on target? In what do you need to continue with steadfastness? Are you serving Christ with toil and perseverance? Then keep on! Are you living a holy and pure life? Then press on! Do you hate sin, both in the church and in the culture around you? Then stay after it! Do you witness for Christ in the face of opposition, ridicule, and loss of reputation? Then keep on!

"Let us not lose heart in doing good" (Galatians 6:9).

Revival occurs when we continue to pursue holiness. It occurs when we continue in the path of obedience. That's where the rubber meets the road.

4. THE LAW OF CONVICTION

Then, sin must be exposed. If we fail to deal with the sin problem in our churches, revival will be thwarted. This occurs through the reproving power of God's Word and the convicting ministry of the Holy Spirit.

Five of the seven churches are rebuked for their sin. The two churches that receive no rebuke—Smyrna and Philadelphia—are the two most persecuted churches. That tells us that persecution purifies the church.

Ephesus needed to deal with their diminishing love for Christ. They had left their first love (Revelation 2:4). Pergamum needed to confront their doctrinal compromise (2:14). Thyatira needed to address their moral compromise (2:20). Sardis needed to be purged of their spiritual deadness (3:1). And Laodicea needed to have their lukewarmness toward Christ changed (3:15-16).

Coldness toward Christ was the problem in Ephesus, Sardis, and

Laodicea. *Compromise* toward His Word was the issue in Pergamum and Thyatira. Those are the two primary sins that must be exposed in the church—*coldness* toward Christ and *compromise* toward His Word.

Sin can only be exposed by God's Word and His Spirit. When walking into a dark basement and flicking on the lights, roaches may be suddenly exposed. They begin scurrying for a dark hiding-place. So, God's Word—a brightly shining lamp and light (Psalm 119:105)—exposes secret sins concealed in the dark recesses of our hearts. If revival is to come, we must clean our hearts of every known sin.

Sin means falling short of the divine standard—the glory of God (Romans 3:23). Though some may fall short more than others, all fall short. The church must call sin sin and not alter the divine standard.

> *Man calls it an accident;*
> *God calls it an abomination.*
> *Man calls it a blunder;*
> *God calls it blindness.*
> *Man calls it a chance;*
> *God calls it a choice.*
> *Man calls it a defect;*
> *God calls it a disease.*
> *Man calls it an error;*
> *God calls it enmity.*
> *Man calls it a fascination;*
> *God calls it a fatality.*
> *Man calls it an infirmity;*
> *God calls it an iniquity.*
> *Man calls it a luxury;*
> *God calls it leprosy.*
> *Man calls it a liberty;*
> *God calls it lawlessness.*
> *Man calls it a mistake;*
> *God calls it madness.*
> *Man calls it a trifle;*
> *God calls it a tragedy.*
> *Man calls it weakness;*
> *God calls it willfulness.*

5. THE LAW OF CORRECTION

How is sin cleansed and removed from a church?

To each of these five churches, Jesus offers one and the same solution. For each of the five sins, there is but one answer—*repent!* Confession of sin (1 John 1:9) is implied and implicit in repentance. But our Lord's emphasis here is upon repentance, not confession. Confession is only an initial step, while repentance goes all the way. Confession washes off our dirt, but repentance pulls us out of the mudhole.

Revival occurs when we get our lives cleaned up. Each of us has sin that must be washed away, and only confession and repentance will allow Christ's blood to do that.

Repentance means a change. It is a turning away from something with deep sorrow and beginning to move in a new direction. Repentance is a change of mind, a change of heart, and a change of will that completely changes a person's life.

So, to Ephesus Jesus says, "Remember therefore from where you have fallen, and *repent*." To Pergamum He says, "*Repent* therefore; or else I am coming to you quickly." To Thyatira He laments, "I gave her time to *repent*; and she does not want to *repent*." To Sardis our Lord warns, "Remember therefore what you have received and heard; and keep it, and *repent*." And to Laodicea He says, "Be zealous therefore, and *repent*" (Revelation 2:5, 16, 21; 3:3, 19).

Too often Christians choose to sweep their sin under the carpet and fail to deal with it. In such cases—where there is no repentance—the fires of revival are quenched.

A college freshman once went to his dorm laundry room to clean his clothes. His dirty clothes were bundled up in an old sweatshirt.

But he was so embarrassed by how dirty his clothes were that he never opened the bundle. He kept them stuffed inside his filthy sweatshirt so no one else could see them.

He then pushed the wadded-up bundle of filthy clothes into a washing machine, threw in some detergent, and started the machine. When the washer stopped, he took the huge bundle out and pushed it into a dryer.

When the dryer stopped tumbling, he took the still unopened bundle back to his dorm room. As he unpacked his sweatshirt, he discovered that the clothes had gotten wet and then dry. But not clean.

The same is true, spiritually, with our lives. If we keep our sins safely concealed in a little bundle, we will never get clean. As God convicts us of sin, we must bring them before Him. We must confess our sins and then repent of them. Only confession of sin and repentance allow God to clean up the dirty laundry of our lives.

John MacArthur was recently in Russia, ministering to the churches there. He was preaching in a worship service. His was the *third* sermon of the morning service. (That's not atypical in Russia. They usually have three sermons!)

At the conclusion of his sermon, MacArthur sat down. An elder of the church then stepped to the microphone and asked very simply, "Does anyone want to *repent*?"

For an hour and forty minutes, the congregation watched as one person after another walked to the front and fell to his or her knees and—with the microphone held to their face—verbalized their repentance. Publicly, humbly, with brokenness and contriteness, the church repented.

This is what Christ calls for. Wholehearted, life-changing repentance. When our sin is exposed by the preaching of the Word, we, too, must repent.

6. THE LAW OF ANTICIPATION

Finally, we must look into the future and see what awaits us in heaven. Revival occurs when we begin to live for the world to come, not for *this* world.

Each of the seven letters concludes the same way. They end by calling the church to look ahead to the day—that final day—when we shall enter into Christ's presence in heaven—either by death or at His coming. Jesus ends each of these letters by giving us a picture of the glory that awaits us in heaven.

This is the final key for revival. While we live *in* this world, we must not be *of* the world (John 17:11). We must be preoccupied with the world to come. We must be heavenly-minded. Unfortunately, we are often so earthly-minded that we are no heavenly good.

Paul wrote, "Set your mind on the things *above*, not on the things that are on *earth*" (Colossians 3:2). Truth is, we must be heavenly-minded if we are to be earthly good. Consequently, Jesus concludes each of his letters with a strong appeal to set our mind on heaven.

So, to Ephesus Christ writes, "To him who overcomes, I will grant to eat of the tree of life, which is in the Paradise of God." To Smyrna He says, "He who overcomes shall not be hurt by the second death." And to Pergamum He says, "To him who overcomes, to him I will give some of the hidden manna, and I will give him a white stone, and a new name written on the stone which no one knows but he who receives it" (cf. Revelation 2:7, 11, 17).

Looking ahead to heaven, Jesus writes to the church at Thyatira, "And he who overcomes, and he who keeps My deeds until the end, to him I will give authority over the nations; and he shall rule them with a rod of iron, as the vessels of the potter are broken to pieces, as I also have received authority from My Father; and I will give him the morning star" (Revelation 2:26-28).

To Sardis, Christ says, "He who overcomes shall thus be clothed in white garments; and I will not erase his name from the book of life, and I will confess his name before My Father, and before His angels" (Revelation 3:5).

To Philadelphia Jesus speaks thus: "He who overcomes, I will make him a pillar in the temple of My God, and he will not go out from it any more; and I will write upon him the name of My God, and the name of the City of My God, the new Jerusalem, which comes down out of heaven from My God, and My new name" (Revelation 3:12).

To Laodicea our Lord says, "He who overcomes, I will grant to him to sit down with Me on My throne, as I also overcame and sat down with My Father on His throne" (Revelation 3:21).

We must be constantly looking forward to the glories of heaven. We are to be preoccupied with the tree of life. Escaping the second death. Hidden manna. A white stone with a new name on it. Authority over the nations. The morning star. White garments. A permanent record in the book of life. Our confession by Christ in heaven. A pillar in the heavenly temple. Receiving the name of God. And the name of the new Jerusalem. And Christ's new name. Sitting down with Christ on His throne.

Our Lord wants us to look ahead to eternity when these future blessings will become ours. When our mind is set on heaven, our life is elevated to a higher and fuller experience of Christ.

Focusing on heaven ignites our hearts for Christ. It purges our hearts of sin—especially worldliness—and turns our hearts from this world toward Christ.

I want to say again, too many churches are focused upon acquiring the material riches of this world. They preach prosperity and insist that people get rich in this world. But our Lord's focus was just *the opposite!* He redirects our hearts to consider the vast spiritual inheritance that awaits us in the world to come.

These are the six laws of revival, each drawn from our Lord's letters to the churches of Asia Minor. They reveal how every church must wake up and answer Christ's call. Here is how a spiritual awakening can sweep through the churches of our land. Here's how revival will come—preach the Word, exalt the Lord, encourage holiness, expose sin, call for repentance, and focus on eternity.

God knows, we need revival. These are the steps that lead to a fuller experience of the presence and power of Christ in our churches and personal lives.

Jesus Himself said so.

It was His *final call.*

THE GAME'S OVER

It's time to stop playing games in church!

Too many churches are playing *Monopoly*. Winning in this game is determined by how much money and property the church can acquire. Budgets, buildings, and buses become the way we keep score.

Other churches are playing *King of the Hill*. Winning is equated with a struggle for the internal power structure of their church or denomination. Whoever can step over people to get to the top declares himself the winner. This is a board game—unfortunately played on church boards.

Still other Christians are playing *Trivial Pursuit*. Winning in this game is defined by the recall of obscure facts about the Bible that have not yet changed their lives. As Vance Havner once said, "They cross all their 't's and dot all their 'i's—but they misspell the word."

There are countless other games that churches are playing today. But winning these games is not what determines success in the church. All such childish playing occurs when a church is spiritually bankrupt of the real thing—*revival!*

This is no time to play church.

God, send us revival!

These laws of revival must be put into practice in every church across the land. Every pastor, church leader, and Christian must put these into practice in his or her daily life. Exposit the Word. Exalt the Lord. Encourage holiness. Expose sin. Exercise repentance. Emphasize heaven. These laws, Christ says, usher in His receiving presence in the church.

The call must go out!

It must go out far and wide.

The church's need for revival has never been greater. The night has never been darker in America. The hour has never been later. The time for the return of Christ is upon us.

The final call of Jesus Christ—recorded in His seven letters to the seven churches—must be sounded to every church across the land. This call is His last message to the church. It is a call to wake up. A call to repentance. A call to holiness. A call to stand and fight.

From the churches of America, the call must sound forth. From every pulpit, the call must be heralded. And in every pew, the call must be heard and answered.

A new army of believers in this generation must answer our Lord's call. The call must go out in the night. Covers must be thrown off. Candles must be lit. Curtains pulled back. Muskets grabbed. And horses mounted.

The call must be sounded throughout America today.

Loudly.

Clearly.

Urgently.

The call must go out!

Final Call
was typeset by the Creative Services Department
of Crossway Books, Wheaton, Illlinois.

Compositor: Jenny Kok

Manuscript editor: Ted Griffin

Art Direction: Mark Schramm

Text Design: Jenny Kok

The text was set in 11¼ point Bembo
justified to 25½ picas width
The leading is 13½ points